DAVID CAMPBELL was born in E⟨ ⟩
in the story- and song-rich North-⟨ ⟩
a lifelong passion for poetry and th⟨ ⟩
graduated with Honours in English ⟨ ⟩
He then worked with BBC Radio Sc ⟨ ⟩ years devising,
scripting and directing a wide variety of radio programmes. He has
also reviewed books and drama extensively in the Scottish press
and has published poems and short stories in the Scottish literary
magazines *Chapman*, *Words* and *Textualities*. He co-wrote the children's book *The Three Donalds* (Scottish Children's Press, 1996),
wrote two collections of stories – *Tales to Tell* I and II (St Andrews
Press, 1986 and 1994) – and is at present working on a literary ceilidh
of the great traveller Duncan Williamson. As a popular ambassador of
Scottish lore and literature, he has toured worldwide with his
repertoire of talks and stories. He currently lives in Edinburgh.

Out of the Mouth of the Morning

Tales of the Celt

DAVID CAMPBELL

Edited by Linda Williamson

Luath Press Limited
EDINBURGH
www.luath.co.uk

First published 2009

ISBN: 978-1-906307-93-6

The publishers acknowledge the support of

towards the publication of this volume.

The paper used in this book is recyclable. It is made from
low chlorine pulps produced in a low energy, low emission manner
from renewable forests.

Printed and bound by
Bell & Bain Ltd, Glasgow

Typeset in 10.5 point Sabon
by 3btype.com

Contents

Acknowledgements

PERMISSION HAS BEEN granted from Mr Archie Bevan, literary executive of the works of George Mackay Brown, to include 'Betty Corrigall', first published by John Murray in *Northern Lights: A Poet's Sources*. We are grateful to Sir Maxwell MacLeod for personal stories and to Neil Macgregor for editorial assistance. The Literary Department of the Scottish Arts Council gave financial assistance in 2006 which made research possible for this collection of Celtic tales.

Preface

ON A HILLSIDE weary from the hunt, Finn mac Cumhaill and his followers were at rest. 'What,' asks Finn, 'is the sweetest music?' Each according to his nature and loves gave an answer. They in turn put the riddle to Finn. 'The sweetest music,' said he, 'is the music of what happens.' Thus he expressed in hazelnut brevity and wisdom the essence of that Celtic sense of living in the moment, and the knowledge that a veil but tissue-thin separates human consciousness from the consciousness that imbues every creature, tree and form. As the early folklorist T.W. Rolleston wrote, 'The Celt did not systemize the unknown, but let it shine for a moment through the opaqueness of this earth and withdrew the gleam before we knew what we had seen.' In this world the riddle is the natural king, for it yields but oblique glimpses of fleeting reality. It is, as well, the whetstone that sharpens the mind and tests insight. It is the IQ test of the Celtic world, and central to many tales of the hunt, the battle, the heart, the game of chess or death.

For death itself is but a door. Schools of druidry taught the immortality of the soul and the interchangeability of human and animal forms. Hence the power in the mythic tale of the totemic black boar of Celyddon, the emblem of the Campbells today. To the destiny and death of this enchanted boar Diarmad the legendary seed of the clan Campbell was bound by a fatal curse. This sturdy tale opens the first part of our work, Lore of the Fianna.

The Fianna was an elite band of hunter-warriors whose task, as a fealty to the high king, was to keep safe from the foot of any invader the shores of Erin and Alba, the ancient Celtic kingdoms of Ireland and Scotland. Theirs was a high code of honour prizing alike skills in battle and the hunt, accomplishments in the arts of peace and worthy behaviour; in particular the care of women and children. Pervading their high deeds is a poetry of gentleness and elegance.

When the Celtic saints arrive in Scotland in the sixth century, part two of this work, the miracles and deeds of their lives have the robust fearlessness of the boar, and seamlessly incorporate the ancient druid rites. With the triumph of Christianity the druidic cult went underground preserved in the leafy undergrowth of Celtic story and song and especially in poetry. Love is a constant in the cross from pagan to saint.

The status of 'saint' was in these times accorded to holy men and women for the goodness, wisdom and spirituality of their lives and deeds. These saints, invariably of high birth, carried an aristocracy of temporal and spiritual authority.

Part three of our triune of storytelling from the Celtic northern kingdoms unfolds two legacies from these far back times, each with its ferocity and gentleness: one, the deeds of the holy men and women; and the other, the lore of the fairy folk. The spirit of the early saints runs through the veins of time to transfuse the towering presence of Lord George MacLeod as spiritual heir of Colum Cille. Like his brother missionary, Lord George carried an aristocratic torch of fiery words and deeds while simultaneously shedding the glow of compassion.

Beings of compassion and vengeance dwell in a parallel world invisible to mortals. They are the sídhe, the hidden folk. These aboriginal dwellers in green Erin, defeated by the Milesian sons of the Gaels fled to their enchanted knowes. This forced exodus resonates through the ages to our own time, to the fate of all the disinherited, the dispossessed of their land. Unsurprisingly they at times work mischief on the usurpers. From many places desecrated by the disrespect and destruction of man the fairy folk are fled. Our Celtic fairy stories are reminders of a primal relationship with the land which we jeopardize at our peril, timely parables for our age which has lost the knowledge of the connectedness of all things.

This ancient world spirit of living connectedness is nowhere better expressed than where the path of our stories goes north – to the work of George Mackay Brown. His utterance, 'We are all indissolubly involved in each other and in the whole totality of human kind, dead and unknown from the beginning to an unforeseeable end,' could have been learned from the schools of the druids.

Here in Orkney, Inse Orc, 'the Isles of the Boars', Picts were established in 300 BC. Concluding the last section of our Celtic stories is one tale of stoic bravery and a blessing from nature, two of our cherished inheritances from these ancient, artistic peoples.

The sources of stories in *Out of the Mouth of the Morning* are primarily and predominantly from the oral tradition and the early written canon of Irish Scottish scribes. A sliver of their complicated history and references is given in the Notes and Resonances by Linda Williamson. Her Glossary gives the origins of Celtic names and words, which the reader may consult as a guide to further exploration of the Celtic languages. The work is a reminder of the spiritual blood line from early times to ours, from the tales of the brave and gentle Celtic hunter-warriors, the legends of Colum Cille, the warrior Christian of the sixth century, to his spiritual and cultural inheritors Lord George MacLeod and George Mackay Brown, and through that doorway to the folk of the otherworld. It is a reminder that we too can see and hear through that door in the wind, hear and see from beyond the veil those wonders that translate into art, music, poetry, dance and story.

As well as having access to versions of stories through great collectors in the past, I have had the luck and privilege of having as friends the great traveller storyteller Duncan Williamson and George Mackay Brown, both of whom generously gave me their permission to retell tales of theirs as a live performance. I first met with Lord George MacLeod when he made a radio broadcast for me in 1982 and subsequently on visits with his son Maxwell. Over the last 20 years travelling the world as a storyteller it has been my aim to be an ambassador of this great pantheon of tales. In that time I have gathered many stories and worked together with highly skilled musicians such as Jennifer and Hazel Wrigley and Celtic masters of tradition as Paraig MacNeil.

The impulse to make of them a book came when the Irish storyteller Claire McNicol, a close associate, and myself were arranging a programme of tales about our common ancestor Diarmad, seed of the clan Campbell. Then through a door in the wind blew Linda Williamson with her myriad literary talents to edit, type, and as a boar muse to inspire completion of this work.

Many of the hero tales and saints' legends originated as ballads, narrative verses from the brown harp of Diarmad. And, in the text below, poetry infuses the stories because they were, in the words of Mackay Brown, 'conceived in simplicity, surrounded by silences'. A little space within the heart: from this heart the channels of creation spread. In that eternal spirit, flyting and friendship gang thegither, and so I hope this book will be for readers that kind of robust friend, one they will wish to tell of to others in the great carrying stream in which I feel privileged to be a passing custodian.

I wish to thank all the people living and dead who contribute to these stories. *Out of the Mouth of the Morning: Tales of the Celt* is an invitation to retell these stories, bring them from the pages into the air again to leap alive into the music of the moment, the sweetest music, 'the music of what happens'. For in the age-old relationship of storyteller and listener is an implicit pact of love, a way of mutual seeing and discovery. In that meeting place is magic that gives glimpses through the veil and wakens hidden possibilities in all of us.

A note on the Scottish Gaelic and Irish which flow through the English text: the Glossary provides lexical and historical information which may be useful as a guide to further exploration of the living oral tradition, storytelling in Ireland and Scotland today.

I

Lore of the Fianna

The Birth of Diarmad

ON A NIGHT without stars it was that Diarmad came through the dark door of birth. In a little forest hut, rough cloth and rushes was his birth bed. Like a soft keening in the wind was the cry his mother let out that brought him into the world. With the first breath of Diarmad a hush fell on the forest. Bear, wolf and wild boar were silent.

The mother of Diarmad was Cróchnat of the burning hair, high of birth and proud of spirit, fierce and fearless before any man. Her husband was the warrior Donn Ó Duibhne, a man dark in complexion and swift to anger. At this time he had struck the child Diarmad and raised his arm in anger against the woman, his wife, with ugly words had put upon her shaming names. For these deeds of cruelty, by the high code of the brotherhood and the command of their leader Finn, he was banished from the company of the Fianna.

It was the custom amongst the sons of the Gaels to foster children to an uncle. Diarmad was fostered under the wise care of his uncle Angus Óg. Angus was old as the oak trees about his house and young as its first leaves at the first breath of spring, for Angus had drunk of the ale of immortality and was of the blood of the god, Dagda. Twenty-one years he had learning in the school of the druids.

In the time of the banishment of Donn, the high spirited Cróchnat of the burning hair, mother of Diarmad, took to her bed a man called Roc the Chief Steward of Angus Óg. By this good man Cróchnat bore a son, half brother to Diarmad. Reared by Angus Óg the two boys learned the skills of battle and the arts of peace. All was well until the day that fate put the destiny of both under a fatal curse. Finn mac Cumhaill with his hunter-warriors, poets and musicians came to visit the house of Angus Óg. Donn, the father of Diarmad, his banishment now at an end, was in that company.

As ever in these sweet days when yet the world was young Angus Óg and his household feasted the guests with the greatest of hospitality. Drink was in the drinking place, meat in the eating place, story, music and song rang under the rafters. The harpist composed a song in honour of the guests and in that song he made verses in praise of the young Diarmad and also his half brother, the son of Roc the Chief Steward:

> Diarmad of the auburn hair is great of spirit
> big is his heart with generosity
> strong in deed and brave in the struggle,
> Diarmad will win the heart of fair ones.
>
> His equal in spirit is the brother of Diarmad
> fearless in the ways of combat
> none will better him in the tussle,
> together the brothers will meet at the dark door.

So sang the harper.

Hearing these words that put such high praises on the Steward's son, and sang him an equal of own son Diarmad, anger leapt in the heart of Donn, and the boar leg bones he was gnawing he threw on the floor. Over these bones two of Finn's hounds fell to fierce fighting, snarling, barking, biting, baring their white fangs.

Diarmad and his half brother scrambled to safety. While the men tried to separate the dogs, the Steward's son crawled for safety between the legs of Donn. Unseen by anyone this man clenched his knees together, cracked and crushed the child's skull and let him fall beneath the feet of the yelping hounds.

When the hounds were dragged away there lay the small body, motionless. His father ran to him and lifted him in his arms and let out a sobbing groan of grief. The child held close to him in his arms, he turned to Finn and said, 'It is your hounds have killed my son!'

And Finn, knowing well his hounds replied, 'If there is mark of tooth or claw upon the child you will have what recompense I can make.'

So they took and looked at the body of the little boy and not a mark of tooth or claw was on it. So now it was known some ill deed was in it and the Steward demanded that Finn seek the wisdom and fathoming runes of the druids in the sacred caves of Cruachain to get the knowledge of who had killed his son.

And this Finn did, asking for a chessboard and water in a basin of pale gold. With these he took himself to the dark cave of the druids to have performed the secret water rites of divination. There the druid priests made their ritual observances. In the gloom sat Finn, until at last from the water in the basin of gold arose a mist, and through that mist shadowy forms, and a vision of the crushing of the little skull and the dark face of Donn. When Finn returned the Steward Roc, in silence, waited for his words.

'Take what recompense you will,' said Finn.

'I will know the name of the one who has murdered my son, nothing less,' said the Steward.

And Finn told the name.

'Then,' said Roc the Steward, 'the matter is not hard to settle. Let Diarmad son of Donn come between my knees, and if they close about his skull so be it.'

At these words the heart of Angus Óg was sore for he loved both of these his foster children. And then like fire blown by the wind Donn sprang forward, sword raised to cut the head from Roc the Steward, but fast as thought can reach to hand Finn stood between them.

Finn's eye was like the sharpest spear point, 'Not swords but words will settle this matter.'

And with words it was that the fate of Diarmad was spoken, for Roc the Steward took into his hand a hazel wand and with it struck the body of his son. At once the child came alive in the form of a wild boar with neither ears nor tail.

Striking this boar once more with the wand the Steward spoke these words, 'I put you under a geis, that in the day of the raven you will take Diarmad with you into the place of ice.'

Once more he smote the boar, which rose charging into the wilds of the forest. Afterwards this boar lived in the thickets of Glenelg, the glen of the hunting.

When Diarmad came to manhood, worthy was the place he won amongst the brotherhood in the time of Finn mac Cumhaill for his bravery of spirit, his bigness of heart and the love that was in him for women. Great were his deeds and wide his fame in the high days of the Fianna of Alba and Erin. And as the story tells, it was the boar that brought Diarmad through the dark door of death in the end.

Daughter of the King Under Wave

ONE SNOWY NIGHT of winter, the hunter-warriors of the Fianna returned to their dwelling house. They were cold, wet, weary and hungry after a day of hunting when they had got neither fish, fowl nor flesh. Some were huddled for warmth round the fire in the middle of the room, some lay already in the sleep of exhaustion under their woven blankets and coverings of skin. The wind whistled and howled through the timber cracks.

About midnight came three sharp raps at the door and with a flurry of snow entered in a woman, very wild and ugly, and her hair matted, hanging down to her heels. As if by some strange instinct she hirpled to where lay Finn son of Cumhaill, the legendary leader of the Fianna.

In a voice plaintive as the winter wind she whispered in the ear of Finn, 'Let me in, let me in, under your covering of skin.'

But Finn, seeing her so strange, ugly and wild looking, turned away and would not let her in. At that she gave out a wild howl. Next, to where lay Oisín the poet, across the floor she scrambled. 'Let me in, let me in, under your covering of skin.'

And Oisín too, seeing her so strange, ugly and wild, turned away covering his head in the blanket. She gave out a screech wilder than the last and made her way to where Diarmad, most handsome of the warriors lay. 'Let me in, let me in, under your covering of skin.'

'Woman,' said he, 'you are strange to look at, wild and ugly, your hair hanging to your heels, but for all that come in!' And he made room for her under his covering of skin.

'O Diarmad, for seven years have I travelled over land and sea and I never got shelter any night till this night. Let me to the warmth of the fire now.'

All of the Fianna sitting there, seeing her so ugly, wild, unkempt and dreadful to look upon, left the fire. She was not long there when she said, 'Diarmad, let me under the warmth of the blanket with you now.'

'It is asking too much you are,' said Diarmad. 'First it is to come under the covering of skin you ask, then to the fire. Now under the blanket itself beside me you want to be. But for all that come in.'

So she crept under the blanket and Diarmad turned and made a fold of it between them. But he was not long sleeping till he woke, and looked at her, and saw lying beside him a woman great in beauty.

He called softly to the warriors of the Fianna, 'Is this not the most beautiful woman you ever saw in all the world, in all your days?'

'It is,' they said. And gently they covered her up and let her sleep.

In the half-light of morning she stirred and said to Diarmad, 'Where would you like to see the best house built that ever was built?'

'Why I would have it built on the hillside yonder in the Glen of the White Deer.' When the sun rose out of the mouth of the morning, in came two men of the Fianna. A great wonder was on them.

'On the hill of the Glen of the White Deer,' they said, 'we have seen a great house, where there never was one before.'

'Go to the house you have chosen,' said she to Diarmad.

'I will go, if you will come with me,' he said.

'I will come, if you will make me a promise,' said she.

'And what promise is that?' he asked.

'In all the days that we are together, you will not once, nor twice, nor three times mock me with the memory of how it was I looked when I came to you.'

'It is an easy promise, I never will do that.'

So together they made their way to the great house in the Glen of the White Deer. In it was everything they could desire; wild boar, salmon and venison to eat, heather ale, mead and wine to drink and servants to attend them. For three sweet days they feasted, and had great joy in one another.

Then on the morning of the third day she said to him,

'Diarmad, you yearn to be with your friends of the Fianna, your companions of the hunt.'

'Not so, I am well here with you.'

'Go to them. And the food and the drink, my company and the comfort of my thighs will not be the poorer when you return.'

'But what of my greyhound bitch and her three pups, how will they fare?'

'Have no fear for them,' said she.

So Diarmad returned to great welcome with his companions of the Fianna, yet some had the ache of envy in their hearts. For had he not now the fine house on the hill? And had he not the love of the beautiful woman they themselves had spurned and turned away? When Diarmad had made his way from that fine house down the Glen of the White Deer, the woman stood at the door and watched him disappear over the saddle of the hill. As she stood there, the sun was not high, when she saw coming up the glen towards her Finn mac Cumhaill himself.

He came to where she stood at the door, radiant in the morning brightness, and said, 'It is in my mind you are vexed with me, fair woman.'

'Not so,' she smiled. 'Come in and take a beaker of wine with me. It is of the best.'

'I will with pleasure,' said Finn, 'if you will give me one request.'

'What request is there that I would not give you, Finn mac Cumhaill?'

'I ask one of the pups of Diarmad's greyhound bitch.'

'Choose which one pleases you and take it with you when you go.'

And so Finn went in, drank wine with the woman, and when he left took with him a brindled pup of the greyhound bitch. In the half-light at the fall of night Diarmad returned. At the head of the Glen of the White Deer his greyhound bitch came to meet him and let out a great howl. When Diarmad looked he saw the brindled pup was gone. A great anger burned in Diarmad.

Words blazed from his mouth at the woman before the door of the house, 'I took you in when you were ugly, wild, your hair hanging to your heels. If you had remembered that you would not have let my pup be taken from me!'

'That is once!' said the woman.

She turned her back, and Diarmad asked her pardon and so they made their peace and spent the night together in the fine house at the head of the Glen of the White Deer. When the sun shone out of the mouth of the morning Diarmad once more joined his companions of the Fianna and the hunt of the deer on the high hill. At the door once more stood the woman, and coming in the early sun towards her through the Glen of the White Deer came Oisín son of Finn, maker of riddles and master of word craft.

'Welcome, Oisín, greatest of word-makers,' said the woman. 'Come in and drink of wine with me.'

'I will,' said he, 'if you will grant me a favour.'

'What favour would I not grant to the greatest word-maker of the Fianna?' said she.

'I would have one of the pups of Diarmad's greyhound bitch.'

'It is an easy favour,' said she.

And when they had drunk wine together Oisín took with him the white pup of the greyhound bitch. When Diarmad returned in the gloaming time, his greyhound bitch met him at the head of the glen with two loud cries. With two long howls she met Diarmad.

And he saw the white pup was gone and said to his beautiful hound, 'If she had remembered how she looked when I took her in, ugly, wild, her hair hanging to her heels, she would not have let your pup be taken.'

And the woman heard. 'That's twice!' she said and turned away from Diarmad.

Yet they made their peace and spent the night in the house together. Next morning Diarmad returned to his companions of the Fianna. The woman stood at the door of the house. Fleet as the wind, scarcely bending the blades of grass as he ran through the glen towards her, came Caílte the swiftest runner of the Fianna. Him too she welcomed in. He too requested a pup, drank wine and left with the last of the pups of the greyhound bitch. And when the greyhound bitch met Diarmad in the falling dark she gave three great yells, the most terrible that ever were heard echoing in the glen. And Diarmad knew by this his last pup was gone.

Fury like the battle frenzy was in Diarmad and loud he cursed the woman,

'If this woman had remembered herself, hair hanging to her heels, wild and ugly when I met her, she would not have done this.'

And the woman's voice re-echoed down the glen, 'Diarmad, Diarmad, that is three times!'

And Diarmad turned to go into the house but it was gone. And the woman also. In a moment they were gone. Diarmad lay down with his arm around his hound and wept. There on the hillside at the top of the Glen of the White Deer his arm around his greyhound he fell asleep. At the break of the morning he woke alone on the cold hillside. His hound was nowhere to be seen and he vowed he would take no rest until he found them, his hound and the woman. He would search for her if it were over all the world for all of his days.

'I will find out where she is gone,' he said.

So alone through the long lonely glens of the world he set off. Far he searched, long through the day he searched, and still under the light of moon and stars he searched. At last he came to a little stream, dimpled silver in the moonlight, and there lying beside it was his greyhound bitch, cold and still and dead.

There they lay until morning. So great was his love for the hound that he could not bear to leave her. He lifted her on his shoulders and took her with him on his way. Through hollow glens and hilly lands they walked for six long days. Coming to the saddle at the top of a green glen on the morning of the seventh day, he met an old shepherd man.

'Did you see a woman come this way?' he asked.

'I did,' said the old man. 'I saw a woman, the most beautiful I ever saw. She passed this way on the morning of yesterday.'

'And what way did she take?' said Diarmad.

'Yon path to the sea,' said he. 'After that I saw her no more.'

So Diarmad followed the path to the shore. It went no further. There on a rock he sat leaning on his spear. After some time he saw coming across the water a boat, a coracle of skins and a man rowing it. Into this little craft with his dead hound on his shoulders, he sprang. Saying no word the man rowed the coracle over the sea, and down, down below the waves of the sea. At length the man rested on his oars and fell asleep. Stepping from the boat Diarmad found himself on a great plain. It was not long he was walking on that plain when he found before his feet a great drop of blood.

He stooped and into his napkin he gathered this drop of blood and thought, 'This is the blood of my hound.'

Soon he found a second drop of blood and a third each greater than the last. These too he gathered in his napkin. Scarcely had he done this, when looking up, he saw an old woman, unkempt with tousled hair and a wild eye. She was as if in a frenzy, gathering rushes into a great bundle.

'What news have you, old woman?' asked Diarmad.

'Peace, peace,' said she, 'I can tell no news until I have gathered these rushes.'

'Be telling it while you gather them,' said he.

'There is great haste on me,' said she.

'Why this great haste and what is this place?'

'It is Land Under Wave,' said she. 'The daughter of the King Under Wave has come home. Seven years she is enchanted and cannot sleep. A sickness is on her that no doctor can cure or help. These rushes she finds the most comfortable bed for ease and rest.'

'Will you take me where she is this daughter of the King Under Wave?'

'I will' said she. 'I will put you in this sheaf of rushes, rushes over you and rushes under you, and bring you to her on my back.'

'You cannot do this.'

'I can do it,' she said.

At that moment the dead hound fell from the shoulders of Diarmad. Over the body of Diarmad's greyhound bitch the old woman spread rushes muttering in a tongue strange to the ear of

Diarmad. 'I can do it,' she repeated and put Diarmad himself into a sheaf of rushes, some under him, some over him and lifted him onto her back.

Directly before the daughter of the King Under Wave she brought him, set down the bundle and out of it rose Diarmad. 'Come over to me,' said the daughter of the King Under Wave, and Diarmad went to her and kissed her lips and took her hands and they were full of joy. 'Three parts of my sickness you have taken from me, Diarmad, but I never shall be well. For each time of three times that I thought of you I lost a drop of the blood of my heart, the last so great that I thought I would die and so into this sickness I fell and thought of you no more.'

'I have these drops, here in my napkin. Take them and be healed of your sickness.'

'They can do nothing for me,' said she, 'for I have not the one thing in the world I lack. It is the one thing I never will get.'

'What thing is that?' asked Diarmad.

'It is a thing you cannot get, Diarmad, nor any man for many have tried and all have failed.'

'There is not a ridge in the crossing of the edge of the whole wide world that I will not travel to get it. What is it that is so hard to find?'

'It is three draughts of water taken from the golden cup of the King of the Plain of Wonder and no man will ever get it.'

'Tell me where is this place?'

'Not far from the border of this land it is, but there is a little river that runs in between and you would be sailing on that river in a ship for a year and a night and the wind behind you, and you would not reach the shore of that place.'

'I will reach it,' said Diarmad.

Diarmad was not long walking when he found that river, but could in no way find a way to cross it. Then he saw, standing in the middle of the river, a wee reddish man.

'You are in dark straits, Diarmad of the Fianna,' said the reddish man. 'Here, put your foot in the hollow of my hand and I will bring you across. You seek the chalice, the golden chalice from the King of the Plain of Wonder. I will go with you.'

Diarmad put his foot in the hollow of the red man's hand and he stepped from there onto the further shore. Together they journeyed until they came to the palace of the King of the Plain of Wonder.

There at the gates Diarmad cried out, 'Let there be sent out to me the golden chalice of the king, or his champions I will meet in battle!'

And on that day the king sent against Diarmad two times eight hundred fighting men and at the fall of dark not one of them stood against Diarmad. On the second day against Diarmad came two times nine hundred fighting men and at the fall of dark not one of them stood against Diarmad.

On the third day the king himself stood at the gates, 'From what place do you come that has brought this destruction on my men?'

'I am Diarmad of the Fianna!'

'Pity,' said the king, 'you had not told me so. Seven years before you were born a great seer told of your coming. What is it that you wish?'

'The golden chalice of healing,' said Diarmad.

'That is not a hard thing,' said the king, and brought the chalice and put it into the hands of Diarmad. With it Diarmad returned to the red man who waited at the river.

'With this,' said the red man, 'I know you wish to fetch water from the well of life to heal the daughter of the King Under Wave, the woman you have given your love to. I will tell you the signs that will take you to the well;

> There fill the chalice
> and when you come where she is
> into the chalice put one drop of the blood
> and she will drink, and one drop
> and she will drink, and one drop
> and she will drink.

And with the third drop of blood her sickness will be gone, and gone from your heart will be the love you have for her.'

'That love will not go from me.'

'It will go,' said the little man, 'make no doubt of it.'

At these words, Diarmad was silent.

'The king will offer you a place in his kingdom and great riches. Take nothing. Ask only for a ship for your returning to your companions of the Fianna. And do you know what it is I am? '

'I do not,' said Diarmad.

'I am the messenger from beyond the world to help you because your heart is hot to come to the help of another.'

And Diarmad did as he was bid. At the third drop the daughter of King Under Wave was healed, and with that drop the love for her left his heart.

'Diarmad, Diarmad,' she said, 'your love is gone from me.'

'It is gone,' he said.

The palace was filled with music for the healing of the daughter of the King Under Wave and the king offered Diarmad riches and jewels and a place in his kingdom. Diarmad asked only for a ship and from the Plain of Wonder he came away. And the passing of that time was one year and one night.

It was a snowy night of winter that he came through the door of the house of Finn, where lay his companions in sleep. Great was their rejoicing at the return of Diarmad, Diarmad most handsome of warriors, Diarmad of generous heart, Diarmad friend of women. Seven days was the feasting and if the last day of it was not the best it was not the worst.

House of the Quicken Trees

IT IS MANY NAMES that Diarmad had, for was he not the handsomest and bravest of men in the wide worlds of Erin and Alba! And time and times the hunter-warriors of the Fianna had good cause to be grateful to Diarmad Ó Duibhne.

It chanced that Finn, and Goll, and Conn at their hunting came across the son of the King of Lochlan, and he, in disguise of a fair young warrior, offered these great men of the Fianna hospitality in his house in the Quicken Trees. Finn himself he enticed by offering a contest of riddles; Finn who prized himself for wit could not refuse.

'I will put to you riddles that you cannot unravel,' said the sly king's son.

Finn laughed. 'Try on,' said he.

'A great army sweeps over the plains, the army having no horses but gathering the sweetest treasure?'

Again Finn laughed, 'This is the stuff for children. It is an army of bees gathering the treasures from flowers to make honey.'

'What then,' said the dauntless trickster, 'a woman of Ireland without feet and yet she runs faster than the swiftest horse?'

'Aye,' said Finn, 'the woman is the River Boyne, no feet for sure and if she runs slow she never stops and so outruns the fastest horse.' Not a riddle had the lad but that Finn, swift as a hawk falls on his prey, found the answer.

'Come then to my House of the Quicken Trees' said the youth. 'I will have ready a feast that will be a story for your telling, aye, and riddles you will not answer.'

In they went, and astonishment was in their eyes for all things in that house were of the greatest beauty their eyes had ever seen. The walls were of every colour, the floor bedecked with coverings from far lands and a fragrance from the smoke of the fire was delicious to their breath. There they sat, their eyes dazzled, their senses in a whirl.

'It is a wonder,' said Finn, 'for such a house of great finery to be in this place.'

'There is still a greater wonder,' said Goll mac Morna of the one eye, 'for that fire that but a moment since was so pleasing in its fragrance now gives off the vilest stench that ever was at my nose.'

'And an even greater wonder,' said Caílte, the swiftest runner of the Fianna, 'these walls that but a moment since were of colours fine are now but rough wattled boards.'

'And a greater wonder than that,' said Oisín the Poet: 'where there stood at the walls but a moment since seven high doors there is now but one small door and that one shut.'

'And yet there is a greater wonder still,' said Conn of the Hundred Battles: 'where we sat on soft patterned coverings we now sit on bare ground, and that ground hard as iron and cold as ice.'

At that he tried to rise but could not stir, nor could they all, for an enchantment kept them as if each one was stuck fast and turned to stone. As if echoing from afar they heard the mocking laughter of the young fair warrior. By his treachery they were brought to this pass. Finn then, by his gift of divination, put his thumb to his tooth and thus discerned that outside, their enemies were gathering to make an end of them.

'Sound the music of the borabu!' he commanded, and from his cold lips Oisín blew the great hunting horn of the Fianna. So it was that the followers of Finn, hearing the sorrowful music of the borabu which was a geis that they must obey, came storming at the army of the King of Lochlan's son, but to no avail. Well as they fought the Lochlan army was gaining victory.

Diarmad was at that time dallying with young women, laughing, joking, teasing. When the shrill horn of the Fianna split the air he sped at once to answer the cry. His great love for Finn transformed into a battle-fury, fierce and terrible as that of the legendary Cúchulainn of old. Fearless and afire, he like a giant flame burned a path through the warriors of Lochlan, kindling the like battle frenzy in his companions of the Fianna so that the blood of every Lochlannach who did not flee spilled red upon the earth. With that very blood Diarmad washed the floor of the House of the Quicken Trees and so broke the enchantment and freed Finn and his company of warriors.

Afterwards at Finn's Dún of the White Walls was great feasting, music, song, verse and dance, riddles, and talk of the riddler of the House of the Quicken Trees and of Diarmad's dauntless deeds in the fray. In the midst of this feasting, Conn the idle, lounging by the walls called out to Diarmad.

'Diarmad, take me over here a piece of that roasted venison!' To him the ear of Diarmad was deaf. 'Ach now,' jibed Conn, 'if it was the sweet voice of a young maiden was asking, your ear would not be deaf!'

For truth it was that as many women loved Diarmad as he himself gave his love to. And so if he was Diarmad the brave, Diarmad the comely, Diarmad the hawk, so oft was he called;

> Diarmad the friend of women,
> Diarmad the wooer of women,
> Diarmad of the *ball seirce*,
> Diarmad of the love-spot.

And that story is for another telling.

The Love-Spot

IT WAS A MORNING of mornings, on a day of days, bright the red dawn and four hunters high on the hill, four hunters in the dew-fresh sunrise, hot in pursuit of a fleet white deer. The hunger of the hunt was on them in pursuit of this white shadow, the elusive milk white hind. And who were these hunter-warriors in the red dawn? They were men of the Fianna, that elite brotherhood whose task it was to keep safe the shores of Erin and Alba, the ancient kingdoms of Ireland and Scotland from the foot of any invader. Wily were they in the ways of war, fearless in the spear-rush, these companions in the swift chase; accomplished these men in the arts of peace, skilled to unlock the riddles of harp and verse and song, these friends fierce in pursuit of the white deer. Yet ever as the hunt closed she eluded them, a glimpse, a white shadow in the sun glint at the trees edge, and she faded as into a mist and was gone.

And these four, the choicest of the brotherhood of the Fianna:

They were Goll mac Morna
fiercest of the fighting men of the Fianna,
Goll of the one eye and that eye
sharper than the eye of an eagle and
he strong in the hunt of the white deer;
they were Caílte
swiftest runner of the Fianna, he whose feet could
race over the meadows of morning without
bending the tips of the blades of grass and
he swift in pursuit of the white deer;
they were Oisín
clever in the word craft, greatest of word makers
greatest of all poets of all lands since the dawn of time,
he who could unravel all riddles and
he elegant in pursuit of the milk white hind;

they were Diarmad Ó Duibhne
most fearless of the warriors of the Fianna,
Diarmad friend of women
most handsome of men
most generous of heart and
he tireless in pursuit of the beautiful white deer.

These four, bent on the hunt in the autumn cold wind, were strong and swift in pursuit of the beautiful white hind. On before them she sped, nimble and elegant through dappled forest, and beyond the treeline she led them. Over crag, and glen, and mountain moorland, the length of the day tireless in the chase they followed, the hunger of the hunt on them.

And ever as they drew near nimbly she flew, flitted through the glitter of the silver birch trees, a wisp of mist before them, she faded. As the sun was dipping, shadows deepening, dark falling, into the gloom of the forest she fled and was gone. They lost her, the beautiful milk-white deer. Night thickening, cold clinging, hopes failing, through the darkness of the forest they peered. They gazed still, and intent, and saw a glow down in the darkness of the trees, a light, and approaching, saw a hut, a strange little house, light shining from it. In the darkness of the doorway stood a man, grey, grizzled, old, an ancient man. He beckoned, welcomed them.

'Honour my house, strangers; and yet, no strangers to me, great warriors of the Fianna!' And each of them he called by name:

Caílte, fleetest of foot in
Erin and Alba, welcome!
And Diarmad Ó Duibhne, bravest and
most handsome of men, welcome!
Old Goll mac Morna, fiercest of the
fighting men of the Fianna, welcome!
And Oisín, greatest in wordcraft,
most skilled of poets, welcome!

Strange to their sight was this ancient man, deep set in his skull his dark eyes, grey his hair, and he bent with great age. They went in and little was there, a fire, a table, and tethered in the far corner a ram; by the fire sitting, a beautiful young woman fresh as the first dew of morning, milk-white her skin. The ancient one bade her prepare food. Swiftly, elegantly she spread the board. They sat to eat. And as they would eat the ram broke its fastenings, snapped its tether, leapt upon the board and pranced amongst the food before them on the table glaring, its eyes defiant. Silent were the warriors of the Fianna.

'Arise, Caílte,' said old Goll, the fierce one, 'rise and fasten that ram to the place it was!'

Swiftly, speedily, sprang Caílte. Dexterously by the horn he seized the ram. But the creature, slate grey his glaring eyes, twisted and hurled the hunter to the earthen floor and stamped his foot upon the breast of Caílte, staked him to the ground.

The eye of Goll was fire, 'Rise, Oisín and take that ram to its place!'

Cunningly, carefully, Oisín came at the ram, with stealth he grasped the horns. He tussled and wrestled, he turned and twisted, but the ram threw him to the floor and placed its hoof upon his chest. Silent was Goll mac Morna.

'Bravest Diarmad,' said old Goll, 'bravest of the Fianna, remove that ram to its place!'

Gracefully rose Diarmad. He grasped the horns, but the ram threw Diarmad into the dust and set its foot upon his breast.

Goll, cold fury in his single eye, arose, 'This beast I myself will tether and tame!'

With his large and mighty hands spread he grasped and gripped fast the horns. The ram bucked and heaved and in an instant threw him on the ground, put Goll under its fourth foot and bleated, as in mockery.

'Ah, great shame,' said the ancient man, 'to see this done to the great warriors of the Fianna.'

And indeed they would not lift their eyes. At this the old man rose. By one hand he took the ram and led it, docile as a lamb and fastened it to its place at the end of the house. Shame was on the four fine warriors of the Fianna, an old man to better the pride of Finn's fighting men.

'Eat,' said the old man, but they had no mind to eat, no stomach for food. 'It is no shame to eat,' said he, but they had a mind only to retire and rest and sleep. 'Then rest,' said the ancient one, 'your place is ready.'

And he pointed to a little door, and to that door they crept. Within they found a chamber, spacious enough, five couches in it. So each lay down. And as they lay to rest the young girl, milk-white her skin, graceful as a hind her walk, came into that same room. The light of her beauty shone on the walls, as if it were the light of a candle. When old Goll mac Morna gazed upon her something in his old thighs stirred. A memory, a yearning, moved and tugged in those hoary loins. And over the floor he prowled to where she was.

'What would you, old man?' said she, 'old Goll mac Morna, what would you?'

'Why, to lie with you,' said he.

'Old man, you had me once a time ago, you never will have me again,' said she, 'return to your dreams.'

Confused, searching his memory of a thousand feastings, old Goll returned to his couch and an old man's hot dreams of bygone times. Then saw Caílte the Swift the bright light of her beauty, and swift as the wind to her side he flew.

'O swift Caílte, what would you?' said she.

'To lie with you.'

'You possessed me once, and little heed you paid me then. Never will you have me again, return to your couch.'

And swiftly so he did. And then the eye of Oisín the Poet drank in the radiance of her beauty. With soft and silken words to her side he crept.

'And what would you, sweet maker of words?'

'Why, to lie with you! You who are more graceful than the hind, fresh as the beauty of the dawn, as morning dew on the grass.'

'Sweet you are with words,' said she, 'time was that you enjoyed me, yet for all your honey words you never shall again. Go!'

And so, bewildered by these words he too returned. What riddle was this? The unraveller had no answer. Then rose Diarmad Ó Duibhne and came to her.

'Diarmad, most handsome of men,' said she, 'what would you?'

'Why,' said Diarmad, 'to lie with you.'

'O Diarmad,' she sighed, 'that cannot be. I belonged to you once, and I never can belong to you again. But Diarmad, friend of women, most generous of heart, come close, come close and I will give to you a gift.' She placed her finger on his brow and there she put a *ball seirce*, a 'love-spot'. 'No woman will ever look upon it, but she will forever give you her love. Now go!'

And so he went. And in the early morning, still deep in shame, hoping to creep in secret out, the warriors of the Fianna awoke. The riddles of the night in their mind, they would have stolen from the hut, but there at the threshold stood the ancient man, eyes set deep within his skull, black eyes.

'You are amazed, great warriors of the Fianna, but let me unlock for you these riddles. You are not shamed. You are indeed the bravest men of all Erin and of all Alba, and no shame is on you. For that ram was life itself.' His eyes grew dark, 'And none,' he said, 'can bind or overcome that force of life, but death. And this fair fresh young woman, who once belonged to all of you, why she, is youth. And her you never will enjoy again!' And so the warriors of the Fianna went on their way.

And this is how Diarmad Ó Duibhne came by the *ball seirce* upon which no woman could gaze, but she would be taken with a quenchless, endless, love for Diarmad. But that was to be for him, as you shall see, both a blessing and a bane.

Diarmad and Gráinne

IN THE CELTIC KINGDOMS of Erin and Alba in those far back times when the world seemed yet fresh and young, there was, as you may know, a mighty brotherhood. They were called 'the Fianna Éireann', as great their fame in the arts of peace as in the exploits of battle. At the time when the fame and deeds of this band were at their greatest, their legendary leader was Finn mac Cumhaill. Finn was a man of Celtic prowess and nobility, the paragon, quick and strong in body as in his mind, tall, fair-haired and handsome still, now that years were coming on him. Deep in chest and broad in shoulder, lofty his forehead and keen as dagger point his eyes. Through the forest he could move, silent as his shadow's self.

Of Finn it was told that he was as fair in judgement to a stranger as to his own son, and fair to his own son as to a stranger. Finn could forgive an injury laughing and yet nurse a grudge till the death of that one who caused it. Far and wide it was famed, 'the door of Finn is the stranger's home,' and of his generosity it was sung:

> If the brown leaves were gold that the wood lets fall,
> if the white wave were silver,
> Finn would have given it all away.

Now from the Fianna at that time the clamour rose that Finn should choose a wife to be the companion of his days and comfort of his nights, and truth it was that in Finn himself the memories of Saba, the mother of his son Oisín, stirred desire for warmth in the loneliness of night. Rare would be the qualities of a woman to match the mighty mac Cumhaill. It was for women, as for men in these far back times, that they were prized not for outward beauty alone, fairness of feature and form, but for inner grace, wisdom, wit and generosity.

Word was not slow to travel in the lands of the Celts that this great leader sought a wife. Many and lovely were those who came from far and wide in the kingdoms of the Celts to seek the coveted hand of Finn mac Cumhaill. And then, some say in reluctant acquiescence to her father's demands, came a woman tall and elegant, dusky fair; her hair, of such beauty, it was said, that she could wake the terror of a tameless love. Silk-soft her voice, her eloquence in song, her grace in dance surpassed that of any woman in Erin. Her name was Gráinne.

When Gráinne came to Finn's Dún of the White Walls it seemed as if for a moment even the breathing of the great deer hounds stopped. To her then were put the riddles, to determine if she had a mind worthy to be the consort of the great leader of the Fianna. These were the riddles put by the wise one of the woods.

'What,' said the druid, 'is more plentiful than the blades of grass?'

'More plentiful,' she at once replied, 'are the dewdrops, for to each blade of grass will be many dewdrops.' This answer pleased Finn well.

'What then,' said the seer, 'is whiter than snow?'

'The truth,' said she without pause, 'is whiter than snow.' This answer pleased Finn well.

'What,' said the wise one, 'is darker than a raven's wing?'

'Darker than a raven's wing,' said she, 'is the door of death, for none return to tell that darkness.' This answer pleased Finn well.

'And what,' said the ancient one, 'will burn more than hot iron on flesh?'

She at once replied, 'More than hot iron on the flesh will burn deceit on the tongue of a friend.' This answer pleased Finn well.

'And what,' said the diviner, 'is swifter than the wind?'

'Swifter than the wind,' and she smiled, 'is the thought of a woman between two men.' This answer pleased and puzzled Finn.

'What,' said the wise one, 'is the most precious jewel?'

'The most precious jewel,' said she, taking thought, 'is a knife; for a knife can keep life in and take it out.' This answer pleased Finn well.

Last, he asked the seventh riddle. 'What is more red than blood?'

'More red than blood,' she said, 'is the face of a worthy man, a stranger at the door, and he no meat or drink to give him.'

'Ah,' sighed Finn, and at once the well of his heart was filled with love, for this touched the inner chamber of the great code of hospitality. Of all women Gráinne's beauty shone brightest and her wit glittered sharpest.

A day was set for the wedding feast, and wild and long was the feasting. All the great warriors of the Fianna were there. Nine thousand warriors attended the marriage of the great Finn mac Cumhaill to the tall and elegant Gráinne of the dusky fair hair; Oisín the Poet, Conn of the Hundred Battles, Caílte the Swift and amongst them, the darling of Finn's heart, Diarmad Ó Duibhne, Diarmad of the generous giving.

In the midst sat Finn mac Cumhaill. On his right side with her two milk-white hounds crouched at her feet sat Gráinne. On his left, Diarmad Ó Duibhne, he who had the strange quality of the *ball seirce*, a love-spot on his brow so powerful that should any woman gaze upon it she would at once be smitten with a deep and quenchless love. This spot Diarmad kept always concealed by a cap pulled low over his brow.

For seven days and seven nights was there feasting and drinking, dance and poetry, music and song. This was the feasting of mighty men and wondrous women, of mighty women and wondrous men. The rafters trembled with the thunder of their laughter, the timber shook to the clash of their drinking vessels. On the seventh day when the feast was at its height the hounds fell fighting on the floor over a bone. Amongst them were the two milk-white hounds of Gráinne.

Into their midst to separate them sprang Diarmad Ó Duibhne. He tore them apart and in so doing dislodged the cap and so revealed the *ball seirce*. And who should gaze on that love-spot but Gráinne, the bride of Finn mac Cumhaill. At once heavy was her heart, with love for Diarmad Ó Duibhne.

'It is Diarmad that I love,' sang her heart. 'The warm soul will not be in me unless I am with Diarmad Ó Duibhne, hero of the yellow hair, most handsome of men, Diarmad of the generous heart, bravest of warriors. My soul hungers for Diarmad. By every pulse within my breast, by every strength within my mind, this man will go with me.'

And later, while the clàrsach trembled on the night air and the music rang in the rafters she sat close, close and close to him by the flickering flames of the fire. Her great beauty would have won the heart of any man, her silk-soft voice, the eloquence of her song.

'Diarmad Ó Duibhne, come with me from this place.'

'I cannot,' he said, though joy fluttered within him like the wings of a bright bird, 'I cannot come with you for the bond I have to my wife.'

'Come with me, Diarmad Ó Duibhne, my heart cannot sing without you.'

'I cannot,' he said, though his heart sang like a lark in the high sky. 'I cannot come with you for the bond I have to Finn mac Cumhaill, who is your husband.'

'The warm soul will not be in me unless you are with me. I lay upon you a geis that you will come with me . . . before light steals into this dark night.'

'No,' he said, 'I will go with you neither by day nor by night.'

'Come,' she said, 'we will find a place sheltered from the winds.'

'No,' said he, 'I will be with you neither within doors nor without.'

'Come with me,' she said, 'let us flee from this place.'

'No,' he said, 'I will go with you neither on horseback nor on foot.'

'By your own words and by the geis I lay on you,' said she, 'you *will* come with me.' And indeed when the feast had died into the small hours of the night and when Diarmad Ó Duibhne lay asleep in his little hut there came a tap, tap, tapping at the door and the silk-soft voice of Gráinne, more eloquent than any song, sweeter than any music: 'Diarmad Ó Duibhne, it is I Gráinne who waits.'

And when he came to the door he said, 'I have said I will go with you neither by day nor by night.'

She said, 'It is neither: it is the gloaming hour when the light has not yet stolen into the dark, when night is not yet lost in day.'

'I have said I will go with you neither within doors nor without.'

'I am neither: for I stand under the lintel of the door.' And then he saw that she was neither on horseback nor on foot for she sat laughing astride a goat. 'Come with me,' she said, 'before the first warrior of the Fianna awakes!'

'If I come,' said he, 'we will be safe neither by night nor by day. We can hide in no tree that has not two trunks, seek shelter in no cave that has not two openings. Where we cook we cannot eat, where we eat we dare not sleep, and where we sleep one night we cannot sleep the next for great will be the wrath of Finn mac Cumhaill, swift as wind, swifter his pursuit than the fastest hound hot on the track of its prey.'

'Come with me,' she said, 'darling of my heart!'

And together they fled across green Erin, together looked from the white shore across the dark seas to the grey coast of Alba, the ancient Scotland. And hard was the voyage on that sea by oar and by sail, past the islands of Jura and Islay, the rocky coast of Kintyre, through the treacherous current of the Corrievreckan, beyond the blessed isles. And then to the shores of Alba they came, fled through the forests of Kintail, passed the five sleeping sisters, crossed the high bealach of Màm Rattachan. By day and by night they fled:

> Where they cooked they did not eat
> where they ate they did not sleep and
> where they slept one night they did not
> let sleep fall upon them the next; they did not
> pull the foliage of a tree round them to hide but it had
> two trunks, nor sheltered in the
> darkness of a cave but it had
> two openings.

At last they came to Glenelg in Scotland, the glen of the hunting. And there not rustling a leaf, not cracking a twig, not bending a blade of grass they ran and came fast and safe into the glen. Into a place sheltered from the wind they came and there felt safe, for in that glen was a mighty boar, a wild and mighty boar, custodian of the glen of the hunting renowned for its venom. This creature had neither ears nor tail and eyes that burned like the Beltaine fires. The bristles of the boar were the length of a foot, its great tusks the length of a man's arm. None came to that glen for fear of this creature. No warrior had fought that beast and lived; for as much as a touch of the black bristle took a man through the dark door of death. So silent they went by with all the secret skills of the Fianna, and high in the glen they found a place of shelter from the wind.

With his forefinger Finn touched his tooth and its source of wisdom took his inner eye to where they were. The speed of his pursuit was the fury of his anger. He commanded the borabu to sound, the horn of the Fianna. From all directions in green Erin came his warriors in answer; the shrill note, a geis none could refuse, no warrior of the Fianna deny. And round the fury of Finn they gathered, the mightiest of men. And across green Erin they made their march. In the heart of Finn, treachery burned like hot iron. He wished to see the ribs of Diarmad split with a knife and his red blood spill on the green green grass. He prayed for the dark door of death to take them, Diarmad and Gráinne. Across green Erin over the dark sea, through Kintyre, past the sleeping sisters of Kintail he followed them until he too came to Glenelg, the glen of the hunting, the glen of the wild and venomous boar. Such was the poison in his heart, the resentment at the treachery of Diarmad and Gráinne that when he came to the glen of the great black boar it seemed the very monster of his own jealous rage.

'I will kill this boar,' he said, 'with my own hands.' He matched its poison with his own,

'I will have it dead.' And then as he looked about him, down by the little river he saw shavings of wood floating. He bent down and picked one from the water, held it between his thumb and forefinger and he said, 'This is the work of Diarmad Ó Duibhne. I know the carving of his hand.' And he sounded the Dord Fian, and through the glen sang the wild call.

Far and high in the glen, in the forest Diarmad heard, and hearing he turned to Gráinne and said, 'It is the hunting cry of the Fianna, of Finn mac Cumhaill himself, for answer I must go.'

'The call is a lie,' said Gráinne.

'It is no lie. I must go.' Again the shrill cry rang through the glen.

'If you go you will never return.'

Once more the cry. And for answer he ran, tumbling his footsteps down by the river, and came to the foot of the glen and stood before his old friend and leader, Finn mac Cumhaill. And when they looked into one another's face tears glittered like dewdrops in their eyes. And when Finn saw the face of Diarmad he was filled with love and compassion; he could not believe that this man ever would betray him. And yet the journey, his burning resentment over seas and through lands, searching! The black poison seeped through him. He wished to see a knife, a black knife, split the ribs of Diarmad and spill out his red heart's blood on the green green grass, take him through the raven dark door. Looking into the face of Diarmad he had no heart for this and yet he wished him dead.

'Diarmad Ó Duibhne, handsome warrior,' he said, 'often we have fought together side by side and you were loyal to me.'

'I saved your life.'

'And now,' said Finn, 'are you yet loyal to me?'

'I never broke my bond,' and he looked a naked look straight into the eyes of Finn mac Cumhaill.

A shadow dark as the raven's wing flew across the eye of Finn. 'Would you,' he said, poison in his words, 'to show that loyalty, hunt the great boar of Glenelg for me?'

Finn saw a thin knife of venom enter the flesh of Diarmad and at that moment a raven's shadow flickered across the place where they stood face to face. Like ice, a chill of knowing shivered in the mind of Diarmad. Well he knew this boar of deadly poison in its bristle, knew no warrior had returned from the hunting of that beast; he knew the geis that thirled and twined his time of dying to that of the enchanted boar. And now it was as if he knew the time of meeting at the dark door had come.

Without a moment's flinching, he looked into the eyes of Finn and said, 'I will for you, hunt and kill this boar.'

And at once he took himself into the forest and the warriors waited: Oisín the Poet, Caílte the Swift, Oscar of the wild words, Goll mac Morna, and Finn himself. They waited for the death of Diarmad, and overhead flew two black birds. And then they heard a thunderous stampeding and crashing in the undergrowth, a furious snorting and then, echoing through the glen, a thin wail, a scream in the silent afternoon, high and shrill. And . . . silence.

When Finn and his followers traced the track through the forest onto an open grassy space, there, like the keel of a black upturned boat, lay the boar, black blood oozing from its side onto the green green grass. And there, Diarmad Ó Duibhne, unscathed, unharmed, fresh as morning dew on blades of grass. Finn gazed at him once more, joy and pain at war within his breast until once more resentment filled the well of his heart, black poison. Once more he wished to see him dead.

'Measure the boar along its length.'

The dark thought saw the dark bristles as Diarmad Ó Duibhne measured the boar's length from snout to tail. 'It is seventeen feet,' said Diarmad in wonder, 'seventeen feet.'

'Measure closer,' said Finn, 'I cannot think it is as much,' hot iron burned the flesh in the heart of Finn.

Once more, closer to the deadly bristles, Diarmad measured. 'Seventeen feet,' he said. 'For certain, seventeen feet.'

'Measure closer,' said Finn mac Cumhaill, and Diarmad barefoot measured.

The venomous bristle entered his heel and he fell at once upon the ground, the blood draining from his face, the poison seeping through his body. Cold horror gripped mac Cumhaill, for looking into the eyes of Diarmad the yellow haired, most generous of hearts, he saw no deceit. Once more Finn's heart filled with love.

'How can I help you, Diarmad, bravest of the Fianna?'

'The chill of death creeps on me,' said Diarmad, 'but all men know that you can heal even the dying by the power of healing in your hands. If you but cup your hands with water from the well it will save me, even now.'

And indeed Finn knew that in his hands was a healing and so

he ran to the well and love took his footsteps back fleeter than the hind in flight on the hill, but as he ran – the dark thought, the dark knife, the dark resentment – his fingers opened and the water fell to earth. When he returned, pale was the face of Diarmad, fast was his breath, life flickering from him, the chill of death creeping over him. When Finn saw his friend, without a word he ran back to the well, love in his footsteps, cupped his hands with clear water and came running back – but once more – Diarmad, Gráinne, deceit, betrayal. His fingers opened and the water fell on the earth.

But when he came and saw his friend, and looked into the eyes of Diarmad, the light fading from them, he saw only truth like the white snow glittering on the far mountains. He looked at him and saw such innocence that he ran to the well, took water and returned, his hands cupped full of healing clear water. But then dark was his pain, for Diarmad lay still as stone. Diarmad, most brave and most generous of the warriors of the Fianna lay still and beautiful in death. Finn wept for his friend.

And the little band made its way up the river, up the river to the place where Gráinne and Diarmad had lived. And when they came to that place deeper was the anguish for Finn. There stood Gráinne, straight and proud and pale.

'He never broke his bond,' she said. On one side of the river was the little hut of Diarmad, and on the other the little house of Gráinne.

And then with Gráinne they returned to the burial place at the foot of the glen. There they dug a grave for the great warrior. Loud and bitter then were the cries of lamentation in the glen of the hunting, but none more filled with pain than the soft keening of Gráinne, like the tearing of soft silk. Great tears fell down her cheeks as if to follow Diarmad into the grave. Her face grew pale, her lips bloodless.

In a silent circle stood the warriors of the Fianna and with their shields moved the soft earth into the grave of Diarmad. At one end stood Finn, at the other Gráinne. She raised her eyes and looked into the eyes of Finn, hard and long, and no man knew the meaning of that look. A shadow fell. Above them two ravens wheeled in the red rays of the sinking sun, and in the forest a veil misted the eye of the great boar.

Oisín Son of Finn

IT WAS A BLOWY DAY of autumn, the sun dipping, when Finn, his companions and their hounds were returning from the chase, returning to their white dún in the Hill of Allen. In the half-light of the gloaming suddenly a beautiful fawn started up before them. As fluttering leaves before the wind the chase swept after her, this fleet-foot fawn. Swift was the chase yet soon all fell far behind, all but Finn and his two favourite hounds Sceolan and Bran; these dogs he so loved that it was said he wept but twice in his life, and once was for the death of Bran. They were as no ordinary hounds and like flitting shadows pursued the fleeing deer, ever closing on her as Finn saw them vanishing at her heels over a little hill. Coming over that hillock in the glen a great wonder came on Finn. For there lay the lovely fawn, and Bran and Sceolan playing round her licking her face and limbs as they might a master who had come home.

When the companions of the Fianna came up he ordered none to harm her, and the beautiful milk-white hind ran with them to the Hill of Allen playing the while with Bran and Sceolan. Late that same night Finn lay alone when a young woman came to him, the loveliest that he had ever seen.

'I am Saba,' she said, 'the fleet-foot fawn that you pursued this day. For refusing the love of Fer Doirich, the dark druid, I was put into that shape. Through the length of three long years have I lived under this enchantment, held captive, sometimes beaten by the druid's rod, or offered powers or riches if I would be his. At times soft tender words were on his tongue and when always I refused it was a rage of words or blows he gave me. A slave of the dark druid tended me. One day pity came into the heart of that slave. He told me if I could come within the white dún of Finn mac Umhaill the bonds of my enchantment would be loosed. So here I fled running the length of the day. I made no halt till Sceolan and Bran alone were at my back, for they knew my nature to be as theirs.'

Then Finn gave her his love, took her as his wife and she stayed with him. Now not the battle, not the hunt, nor feast had delight for him ,but Saba alone. His life was his flower, wife of the white dún: their love in one another like that of the immortals in Tir nan Òg, the Land of the Ever-Young. Then word came to Finn that the warships of the men of Lochlan were in the bay. It was laid upon the Fianna, a bond, an oath, a geis from the high king that theirs was the task to keep the shores of Alba and of Erin free of invaders.

So go Finn must, and when Saba protested he recalled and spoke to her the great saying of the one-eyed warrior Goll mac Morna when they were once opposed by a mighty host; 'A man,' said Goll, 'lives after his life, but not after his honour.'

So Finn went against the men of Lochlan. In seven days, leading the fierce fighters of the Fianna, he drove the marauders from the shores. On the eighth day swiftly he returned but as he approached the white dún of Allen saw no Saba on the ramparts awaiting him. And coming in he saw the warriors and women with eyes cast down.

'Where is my flower of the white dún, my lovely Saba?' said he.

And this they answered: 'When you were gone to fight the men of Lochlan, Saba was ever looking down the pass for your return. And then we seemed to hear one day the Dord Fian, the Fianna hunting cry blown on the wind, and looking, saw approaching the dún the likeness of you with Sceolan and Bran prancing as is their custom by your side. And Saba wept and laughed for joy and for all we tried to hold her back, she shouted, "I will meet my love, my husband, father of the child that is not born." And she burst running from the dún towards the phantom form, the shadow of yourself that held out arms of seeming welcome. Then she halted like a stricken thing and there came from out of her such a shriek of bitter pain that tears fell from our eyes. The shadow of yourself lifted up a rod of yew and with it smote her thrice; no Saba then stood there but a trembling deer. The shapes of Bran and Sceolan turned to savage dogs. Then like a sudden wind this deer fled three times in full flight for the dún. But each time these hounds of that shadow-man took her by the throat and dragged her back to him. And, Finn, be sure that we made no delay! But rushing from the fortress gate we saw no druid, hounds, woman nor the fawn. They all had gone. Nothing we saw and nothing we heard, but the howl of dogs on every side, the rushing tread of feet on the hard ground and shrieking in the air, and each man thought them from a different place and then they faded in the wind.'

Finn spoke no word, but smote and smote his breast as it might burst. He took himself into the darkness of his inner room, for two days neither ate, nor drank, nor spoke to anyone. And then he ordered the matters of the Fianna as before. But whenever he was not fighting, for seven years was he searching and ever searching through every remote glen and forest and cavern of the land. The only hounds he took with him were Bran and Sceolan and at last his heart lost any hope of finding her again. And to the joy of his companions of the Fianna Finn went hunting as of old.

One day when they were hot in following the chase, they heard the musical baying of the hounds become a fiercesome growling in a narrow hollow of the glen. It was as if they were in combat with some beast. The hunter-warriors of the Fianna came to that place, and there under a great tree, they saw a young and naked boy longhaired and shapely. Round him the hounds bayed and snapped and sought to seize him, but fiercely Bran and Sceolan defended him as if he were their own. At once Finn called off the hounds. But Bran and Sceolan stayed by whining and licking the little naked boy.

They brought him home with them and when by and by he had learned to talk, this is the matter of the tale he told: 'A gentle milk-white hind had been the one companion that he knew. She sheltered him where they lived in a glen with towering cliffs on every side and no escape was possible. Summer fruits and nuts and roots he ate and in the wintertime found food left for him in a cave. A dark man sometimes came to them, spoke to this deer, sometimes gently, sometimes loud and fierce. But always she shrank in fear and he in anger left. Then not long since, the dark one came, spoke long and long, now soft, now loud, and then took up a wand of yew and smote the deer, forced her to follow him, she gazing always backwards forlornly at the boy. He tried to follow but he could not move, cried out with rage and grief, but could not move. At last he fell senseless to the ground and woke there on the mountainside under that great tree. For days he searched for the green hidden valley finding no sign of it. There it was the dogs discovered him.'

Of the dark druid and the hind, his mother, no one knows the end.

Finn looking into the young lad's face saw in it Saba's face. And so he called the boy Oisín 'little fawn'. A great warrior he became, but greater still a maker of songs and tales, a poet. So that to this very day when men tell of the high deeds of the Fianna they will say, 'Thus sang the bard Oisín son of Finn.'

Oisín and Niam

AFTER THE LAST BATTLE that the Fianna ever fought, it happened, on a misty morning of summer, that Finn and his few companions who remained, were hunting on the shores of Lough Gur when they saw riding towards them on a snow-white mare a beautiful woman. Garbed like a queen, a crown of gold was on her head. Around her shoulders and trailing to the ground fell a mantle of oak brown silk set with stars of red gold. Blue her eyes as summer skies and clear as the dew drops on the grass. From every lock of her fair golden hair hung a ring of gold.

> Redder than rose her cheeks
> whiter than the swan upon the wave
> her skin, sweet as honey with red wine
> her lips; silver shod the horse's hooves
> a crest of gold upon its head.

She rode to where Finn was and said, 'Long my journey was and now have I found you, Finn son of Cumhaill.'

'Of what people are you?' asked Finn. 'From where do you come and what purpose brings you here?'

'I am Niam of the Golden Hair, daughter of the King of Tir nan Óg, Country of the Ever-Young'. From thence I came. I never set my heart to any man but one. And therefore I come, for that man is your, son. For love of Oisín I come.'

'And why,' said Finn, 'of all the fair men of your land or noblest princes under the sun, to Oisín?'

'Even to our land of Tir nan Óg spread the name of Oisín, for gentleness and bravery, and for the gold words of his tongue, his harping and his song. These won my heart before the beauty of all other men.' And to Oisín she turned, her voice soft as a breeze in summer rustling the leaves. She spoke as one who has never asked anything but it was granted her. 'Oisín son of Finn, come with me to the Land of the Ever-Young. And there you will have beauty, strength, power, and Niam as your wife. When Oisín gazed upon Niam and heard her voice as she began to speak of Tir nan Óg, not a limb of his body was not in love with her. And he could refuse her nothing. 'Come with me, Oisín, to the lands west of the setting sun.' A magic song was in her voice:

Delightful is that land beyond all dreams
fairer than your eyes have ever seen
a place of fair green meadows of
orchards bearing fruit through all the year,
green green the trees dripping with wild honeydew
crystal clear the tumbling rivers run.
A place it is where beautiful youths
hair the yellow of primrose, and maidens,
skin pure as snow, walk and talk and
mingle in the golden colours of the
setting sun. The hue of the
foxglove is on every cheek. Their
horses are the fairy breed, their
hounds outrun the wind. No one
speaks of mine and thine, mead and wine are
never ending, the feast will never cloy.
Here is no sickness nor pain no
death nor decay, the music of the soft
breeze, the singing of bright
birds carry the ever-young each
night to the sweet oblivion of dreams.

And as the magic song ended Oisín embraced his father Finn. And all the Fianna gazed in wonder and sadness as he mounted the steed and around the maiden twined his arms. And then, as a beacon of light flies across the land when clouds fly across the sun, faster than the spring wind on the backs of the mountain, across the forest glade they sped. And the Fianna were never in their earthly days to see their darling Oisín again.

The wind rose to a howl, the sky grew dark and the sea as if on fire was lit with angry flames. While Niam rode into the tempest fearlessly, above them pillars of cloud glowed red and lightning split the sky. When the white horse and its riders reached the sea the waves opened before the milk-white mare and closed behind them as they passed. And as they rode the wind stilled, the sky lightened, the sea grew soft. The white horse ran lightly over the waves and it was as if the riders passed into a golden haze.

Strange sights appeared glittering in swirls of silver mist, like palaces of ice, blue glittering ice, sunny domes and palaces of shining stones.

> As if borne on clouds or waves
> he knew not what it was
> a host of sparkling men at arms rode past,
> a hornless deer bounded by
> a white hound with one red ear at its heels
> a young maid on a chestnut mare
> a golden apple in her hand and close behind
> a horseman in a purple cloak
> a sword gold-hilted in his hand.

Oisín was amazed at these strange sights and wished to ask their meaning. But even as he meant to ask her Niam said, 'Ask nothing till our journey's done.'

And by and by, and by and by, they approached amidst a meadow green, fragrant and bright with coloured flowers, a palace, marble-white. And from it came to welcome them a hundred warriors, primrose fair their hair, and each one decked in jewelled armaments. A hundred maidens cloaked in saffron and scarlet silks sang a welcoming.

And then the king and queen themselves: 'Ceud mìle fàilte ort, Oisín mhic Fhionn!' (a hundred thousand welcomes, Oisín son of Finn). 'And with our dear daughter, Golden-headed Niam, no delight that heart has ever yearned will you lack, and here you will be ever young.'

Ten days and nights lasted the wedding feast, and if the last day was not the best, nor was it the worst. Thus Oisín and Niam became man and wife.

And Niam bore three children, each one beautiful: the first a boy they called Finn; the next a girl they named Flur nam Ban, the 'Flower of Women', and Oscar the last. And in this land so honey-sweet and full of plenty, three hundred years passed by, which seemed to Oisín but three. Then like a hunger, a yearning came on him to see once more his father Finn, his comrades of the Fianna, the dogs, the hunt, and hear the shrill cry of hounds high on the hills. And so from the king he got word that he might leave.

But Niam said, 'You never shall return.'

'The white horse,' said he, 'will bring me safe again.'

'If once you leave, you never shall return.' Her summer eyes were clouds of tears. 'And heed this: let your foot but touch the ground, and the Land of Youth you never more shall see. You will become an old man, blind and withered, without liveliness or leaping in you. Nor will you find Finn or your beloved Fianna – they are long gone. Now in that green land only are stunted folk led by a holy priest, crowds of clerks and holy men. And I believe we will never meet again through all the length of your days.'

She kissed him. And Niam of the Golden Hair and their three children, golden fair, waved as once more he took his steed from Tir nan Òg across the mystic ocean. It was the last he ever saw of them.

And when once more he came to the lands of men it was as Niam prophesied. Little puny folk worked in the fields and gazed at him in wonder as if he were a giant. And when he asked of Finn and of the Fianna they spoke of how they had heard legends of his name and his high deeds; and how his son, the beautiful and shining one had been enchanted by a fairy queen or stolen to the Land of the Ever-Young. When Oisín sought out ancient hunting grounds and secret places of the Fianna, nothing could he find. And coming from the forest path, where once the Hill of Allen rose with the white Dún of Allen glistening in its midst, nothing there he saw but weeds and nettles, ragworts and chickweed on the grassy mount. And so in grief he knew his comrades and their hero days were gone.

He turned his steed to go away, brushing the teardrops from his eyes which fell upon the old stone trough filled with clear water, wherein his brothers of the Fianna had dipped their hands. Overcome with joyous memories he alit to dip his hands and drink. At once he tumbled to the ground. The white horse swift as the spring wind on the hill's back, galloped away and faded out of sight. And the years came on him as Niam had said: the brave young face of Oisín withered and sagged, clouds came on his eyes; his powerful body shrivelled and shrank in the weakness of great age.

He cried out the names of Finn and Oscar, Caílte and Diarmad, his brotherhood of friends. In despair he howled on the hounds Sceolan and Bran, but only the thin echo of these names returned in the sighing of the wind. Stumbling and half-blind he found a hazel staff to help him walk. Here was the last of the legendary Fianna.

It was in such a way some peasants found him, lost and hungry and alone. They took him to the holy man, and there in Patrick's house he lived, and to the holy priest he told his tales.

Oisín in Patrick's House:
Patrick of the Bells

AND SO THIS OLD MAN, withered and alone, the shadow that once was the golden Oisín was brought to the house of Patrick, Patrick of the Bells, to the house of monks and clerics. It did not suit him well, the way it was he was treated there. Too much of fasting and the drowsy sound of bells; he longed for the days of hunting, for battle, for chess playing, for music and companionship, for listening to the music of wolves through the end of the cold night; and here he was fed on morsels.

Yet one day, as they sat at meat together, Patrick said to him, 'Did ever you see, in your days of the Fianna, the bone of a shank thicker than that?'

The old man laughed, 'We could put that twig of stringy shank through the narrow hole of the bone of a blackbird's chick. Your monks say I am getting food, but I am not. Scraps that would not keep a mouse alive!'

'More than enough you get,' said Patrick, 'a quarter of beef, a churn of butter, a griddle of bread every day.'

'For your skinny monks,' said Oisín, 'enough for their thin voices and scraggy psalms. I often saw a quarter of a blackbird bigger than your quarter of beef, a rowanberry bigger than your churn of butter, an ivy leaf as big as your griddle of bread.'

'Old man, before the face of God you lie!' said Patrick.

Then was great cold anger on Oisín. He went where there was a litter of pups, and bade a serving boy who was his friend nail the hide of a fresh killed bullock to the wall and throw the pups against it one by one. Each one he threw fell down from the hide until he came to the last, and the pup clung fast to it with teeth and nails.

'Rear that one,' said Oisín, 'and drown the rest.' Oisín then instructed the lad, 'Keep that pup in a dark place from the light of day. Let it never taste blood but care for it well.'

At the year's end Oisín was so pleased with the pup he named it Bran Óg 'Young Bran' after the favourite hound of Finn. One day Oisín called the serving boy and bade him come on a journey with him bringing the Young Bran on a chain. And the dim-eyed Oisín, from his memory, directed boy and hound over moor and ben and loch and through glens that the lad had never seen until they came at last to a hidden cave. He told the lad where he could find and fetch three things: a great sounding horn, a ball of iron and a sharp sword.

And when Oisín ran his hands over each of them he said, 'A thousand farewells to the day the Fianna laid you here. Now,' said he to the lad, 'blow the great horn!' As well as the lad could, he did. 'Did you see anything?' said Oisín.

'I did not,' said the lad.

'Blow again, blow harder, louder.' This the lad did with all his might. 'Did you see anything?'

'I did not,' said the lad.

Then Oisín grasped the horn, blew three great blasts. 'What do you see?' said Oisín.

'Three great clouds on the glen, the first a flight of great big birds, the second of ones larger yet, the third the biggest and the blackest the world ever saw.'

'What does the dog?'

'He stares nose to the wind and not a hair of him not standing up!'

'Loose him now,' said Oisín.

Down into the glen rushed the dog, attacking the biggest and the blackest bird. Fierce the fight till Young Bran made an end of the bird and lapped the blood. And that blood put a madness in the hound; for eyes on fire and jaws wide open he came in a rush at Oisín.

'The dog comes mad and raging for us, Oisín,' said the boy.

'Take and cast the iron ball at him.'

'I cannot,' said the lad.

'Then place it in my hand and turn me where he comes.'

This the boy did and as the hound came at him Oisín threw, and into the wide jaws down the throat of the hound it went, so that down the slope tumbled the hound, twisting and foaming and at the foot lay dead. Then they went to where the dead bird lay. Oisín bade the lad with the sharp sword cut off a leg, then open the bird. Therein he found a rowanberry bigger than he had ever seen, and bigger than the biggest griddle, an ivy leaf.

These, the quarter bird bigger than a bullock, rowan bigger than a churn of butter and the ivy leaf bigger than the biggest griddle, Oisín had brought to Patrick and he said, 'You know now, Patrick of the Bells, that I told no lie. And that is what we held to all our lifetime, the truth that was in our hearts, the strength in our arms and fulfilment on our tongues.'

'You told no lie indeed,' said Patrick of the Bells.

Flyting

SUCH WAS THE LOVE for Oisín that his time in the House of Patrick was later recorded by the poets of Ireland. The worthy Patrick took it as his task to bring Oisín to Christian baptism, and so it was that before the sun was out of the mouth of the morning he would be at him even as the bells of matins rang.

'Oisín old man, it is long your sleep is, rise and listen to the morning psalm.'

'Patrick of the joyless clerics and the bells, the cry of the hounds on the hill is better to me than the noise of your schools, the dirge of your psalms.'

'You are old and silly and grey, Oisín, and never heard music so good from the beginning of the world.'

A dry laugh laughed the ancient Oisín, dry as the shrivelled leaves of autumn. 'O Patrick of the closed-up mind, priest of the dried heart, the song of the blackbird in Glen Leiter, the very sweet thrush in the Glen of the Shadows, the sound of boats striking the strand, these are better to me, these sweeter music. The little dwarf that was with Finn, little nut of my heart, the tunes and songs he made put us into sweet dreams. This was better to me, this was sweeter music.'

'Old man,' said Patrick, 'your time is not long for this world. Abjure your pagan ways. The living God is better for one day now than your Fianna for all eternity.'

'I tell you, Patrick of the books, if my son Oscar were here your crosses would be in little bits, and if Conn, wisest of the Fianna, were here not long would your buzzing be in my ears.'

'Your words,' said Patrick, 'put you on the crooked path of pain.' Once more the old man laughed.

'Patrick, if you met in the path on a day of hunting on the high hill, myself, in company with Diarmad of the big heart; if you joined the feasts of venison and mead and wine and song, riddles and harpstrings singing to the empty skies, you would not fester in this dungeon of paltry priests with their scraps of bread and tasteless gruel, their mumbling prayers and joyless song.'

At this the spark of anger was in the eye of Patrick, 'Leave off, old fool, this talk against God's priests. They point you to the delights and joys of heaven.'

Said Oisín, 'The leap of the buck on the high hill, the glimpse of badgers between two glens I would take a thousand times before all your dry mouth can promise of the joys of your heaven. Tell me this, holy priest, will my hound be let in with me before the court of your King of Grace?'

'O shaking old poet, your foolishness knows no bounds. Your hounds will not be let in.'

'How could your heaven be any place of joy with no hounds in it? I would not take any cut of meat but share was given also to my hounds. Bran and Sceolan, the hounds of Finn, their cry on the hill was sweeter than music of harp or pipes. It was the death of his fleet hound Bran brought weeping to the eyes of Finn.'

Patrick's patience with the old man was hard tested now: 'Finn and the Fianna are lying sorrowful on the flagstone of pain. You yet have time to repent and know everlasting joy of company with God.'

'I do not heed you, Patrick of the crooked staves, there is not truth in your words. Finn would not be in your halls of heaven but he found pleasure in it. Better to him the feasting in the mead halls when the hunt is done. If you had been in our company with Finn, Patrick of the joyless clerics and clanging bells, you would not be giving your ear to psalms, nor your knees to cold flagstones of prayer. No man was greater of heart than Finn. It would be no justice for Finn, a heart without envy, without hatred, to be in bonds. Heed me, priest of the cold heart, no one was greater than Finn, king of the Fianna,

Brave in all lands
golden salmon of the sea
sharp hawk of the air
high messenger in bravery and music
protector of women and children and poets
most generous of men.
If the brown leaves falling in the wood were of gold
if the white waves of the sea were silver
Finn would have given all away.

What God would put such a one in bonds of pain? The Fianna
were as people of gold.'

'Is your tongue done with its prattling, old man? If you saw the
people of God at their feasts of plenty, before the Shining Glory,
the Fianna you speak of would be as nothing.'

'Patrick, I tell you,' said Oisín, 'I would rather have the leavings
of Finn's house than a share of your own meals. I and the clerics of
the mass books are two that never can agree. It were great shame for
your God to put locks of pain on Finn, for if God himself were in
chains Finn would lead the Fianna to free him from his bonds.
Now it is sad I am for the time of Finn and the Fianna, for hunting,
for battle, for chess playing, for drinking, for music and companionship and brotherhood, the music of the wolves through the end
of the cold night. My tale is sorrowful. The sound of your voice is
not pleasant in my ears. I will weep: not for God, but because Finn
and the Fianna are not living. I hear the clang of your bells, Patrick;
would it were the shrill call of the Dord Fian gathering our companions for the clash of spear on shield, the hunt on the high hill!'

At that Patrick rose and said, 'We will pray for you, stubborn
as a stone you are,' and he departed.

Left alone in his cold cell Oisín lamented the high days of Finn
and the Fianna.

'What is it I am? A man old in sorrow without playing, without
the voice of the poets, without courting or hunting, two trades that
were my delight. It is long the clouds are over me this night. I, the

last of the Fianna, great Oisín son of Finn listening to the hoarse voice of bells. It is long the clouds are over me this night, pity it is the way I am now.' Some say that in the end Patrick it was who had his way with the ancient Oisín, and others that it was with talking of Finn his last breath was taken.

II

Legends of the Saints

Kentigern:
Birth of the Beloved

A CERTAIN KING LOT of Lothian, a man half-pagan, ruled in the early times of Christian people in this land. His stronghold was at a place called Dunpelder on Traprain Law. Here he ruled with his queen, the stepmother to his daughter Thenaw. From Ireland came a holy nun Monenna, sent by the blessed Brigid of Kildare, sent to establish a convent there. King Lot agreed to let her build it below the craggy hill of his stronghold and was persuaded that it would be a place fitting for the education of a ruler's daughter. Thenaw could learn there; reading, music, embroidery, Latin. These she learned well and from the holy sisters learned the love of bird and beast and tree and fish. And hearing the sound of the stories of the Bible breathed in her ears she became a Christian. To Thenaw the motherless child – the Holy Virgin Mother Mary infused her heart and thoughts and life.

The young girl prayed fervently that she could in every way be as the Holy Virgin. In her purity and innocence she did not see presumptuousness in her desire, for she wished to carry a child for the salvation of the people of Lothian, a child as Mary had carried such a One for the world.

When she was yet a flower scarce grown from the bud, a suitor came to seek her hand. This young and graceful man was Owain, of noble stock of the Britons, son of King Urien of Rheged, the strongest of the northern kingdoms of the Britons. She was fifteen, the prince seventeen.

Her father sought the power in this match, bade her dress to meet the prince who was much taken by her grace and beauty, and asked the king's permission to marry her.

But not the finest words or the choicest gifts of love could incline the young virgin to marry him.

Her reply to his proposal stung him to the quick of his pride, 'I am already promised to a King far greater than you will ever be.'

The king, her father, thought well of this young Owain, both for his grace and spirit, his royal birth, and the power such a match would bring. Thus he spoke gently of his hopes for her happiness. 'Here is a fine young man, handsome in looks, gentle in character, noble in birth, who loves you with devotion – and patience. He is the perfect match!' Endlessly his daughter refused, retiring always to her meditation and devotion to the Blessed Virgin. At last, enraged, thwarted, her father harshly announced, 'Either you shall be handed over to be the servant of the swineherd, or, you marry this young man! Choose!'

The girl said, 'I thank you for the choice, father; I shall serve the swineherd.'

For still in her heart she was sure that to be like the Holy Virgin, a chaste servant in the house of a poor peasant was greater far than to become a queen in the palace of a king. In the company of the swineherd she trudged to his little house in the Lammermuir hills. Only far from Dunpelder did the swineherd say, 'My lady, I and my family follow Christ the Lord; we will do everything to protect you.'

The swineherd showed her every respect. He himself was a chaste man, secretly, too, a Christian. The words and deeds of the good bishop Serf had brought him to believe in and worship the Christ God.

When young Owain saw what her father had done because she would not accept the marriage he was sad, sad at heart, for he loved her. He knew an old and crafty woman. This woman he sent to Thenaw, thinking that now she was so debased living in the hut of a swineherd, working with pigs, that she would long for the life he could offer her, the sumptuous life of a princess.

So the crafty woman came purring words into her ear, 'So sad, you, a royal child, should be in this filthy place with these servant's tasks, looking after pigs!' The old woman spoke of Owain too, of his gentle kindness, his nobility of spirit and of the comfort of the court; but nothing could sway the girl.

'It would be easier to turn the stones into wood, or words to stones than to change her mind,' she told Owain. 'Unless,' said the old woman.

'Yes?' said Owain.

'Unless,' said the crafty one, 'you win her confidence, win her trust. And then, take her, break down that maiden wall. After that she is yours, the fire in the flesh is lit. So it was with me.'

The young Owain was already aflame with desire, 'If I once have her, she will be mine,' said he.

'She will,' said the old woman, a look in her eyes as if she gazed far back through days. Owain was a smooth-skinned and beardless youth. With the help of the old woman, her skills with herbs and dyes, he took on the dress and appearance of a peasant girl.

And thus, passing by from time to time he nodded, and with friendly words passed the time of day with Thenaw, as she tended the swine in the field. And so it was that by degrees he won her simple heart to see him as her friend. One day, unseen, he followed her to one of her secret places, a grassy glade amongst the trees. There beside a stream that sprang from a little fountain often she would come to drink and wash and pray. Lurking there he heard her pray and heard words beseeching God that, like the Blessed Virgin whom she adored, she would bear a child who would become the salvation of the people in this northern land. This put into Owain's mind a clever strategy. Coming into the glade in the guise of the peasant girl as if startled and pleased, he greeted Thenaw.

'My friend, how the day has smiled on me,' he said, 'as if my feet were guided to where you are.'

'How so?' Thenaw replied.

'I have gathered a wood bundle and can by no means get it on my shoulders and my master waits for it.'

'I will help you, surely,' said Thenaw.

Very slow and in a soft strange voice most like a girl's Owain said, 'And if you do, great will be your fortune, your heart's most deep and innermost longing will be yours.'

A deep dark flush of untold joy was in Thenaw; for sure this was an angel's message that told that she indeed would bear a saviour

of her people. She followed Owain as if entranced. He led her to a
grassy sheltered hollow, suited to his purpose. And there front to
front he faced her, clasped her hand and as she began in bewilderment and then dismay to struggle to be free he threw her to the
ground, and while she fought he forced and entered her, and for
Thenaw, day and sunlight faded into blackness. Owain in his dark
force so swiftly entered and took his desire of her, that he believed,
already she had been the swineherd's concubine. And so at once his
desire and what he had called his love for her was gone.

When Thenaw, dazed, with red-rimmed eyes, woke into the haze
and then the brightness of the day she was in a bewilderment. Her
friend, the peasant girl was gone. Of what had happened she had
no memory but from that time within her womb a child began to
form. As her body changed in passing days she called upon the
Holy Virgin and upon the name of Christ and pondered if in some
holy trance an angel had not visited her.

Her pregnancy soon was clear to everyone – spying eyes and
whispering tongues took word to the king. He had been disobeyed
and now his house dishonoured. She had stained his name. Her father
ordered her to be stoned to death, according to the laws of the land
for those highborn, a daughter who had played the whore. Amongst
the executioners none could be found willing to throw the first
stone. Yet not daring to disobey the king's judgment, they brought
her to the top of the Kepduf Hill, by Traprain Law, placed her in a
chariot, where they would let it hurtle down the precipice and take
her to her death. No single one could then be held responsible: at the
top of that hill the rocky cliff falls 300 feet, a sheer descent and certain
death. In the face of death a great clarity came upon Thenaw.

Raising her eyes, her hands, her voice to heaven she said:

> O Holy Virgin, I see in my folly I desired
> what was not worthy to be as you in all things,
> I see the justice in my punishment
> I implore thee, pray to Thy Son, for the sake of my child
> who is innocent save us from this moment of death.'

It is told that as the chariot plunged from the summit she signed the sign of the cross and called out loud and clear the Holy Virgin's name. Down the cliffside crashed the chariot. Waiting, and watching the awful spectacle, stood a group of women friends from the convent. Down it hurtled, grinding, splintering to a halt – and from it bruised, bleeding, but alive stepped Thenaw. Miraculously saved. It is told that in the downward career of the chariot a shaft from the vehicle plunged into the earth and from that place a most limpid fountain gushed, and flows to this day! It is also told that the soft wood wheels of the chariot made ruts in the hard flint stone as if it were of wax, and to this day, too, these ruts remain.

The king's advisers called this 'magic', this great escape. And so the king, to let justice seen to be done, and to avoid the conclusion that his love for his daughter swayed his judgment, heeded them when they said,' If she is worthy of life, give her to the sea. If it is God's will that she lives, so let it be!'

And so the ordeal of the chariot over, she was taken four miles to Aberlady Bay, her sentence – to be put to sea in a boat of one hide without sail or paddle. Aberlady Bay was where fishermen cleaned and gutted their catch of fish. Seagulls screamed overhead and the place stank with rotting fish. It was known as the Shore of the Stench. To this place she was followed by a great crowd of men and women, openly weeping, 'How could a father pass such judgment on his child? It is cruelty to punish twice for the same crime. The judge himself deserves to die for such cruelty!'

She was set adrift in the little coracle of leather, one hide. On the shore the people prayed, 'Let the God who delivered you from death on land save you from death on the water.'

She herself prayed, 'Be Thou the judge, O God, come to my help!'

Meanwhile the king, impulsively and without question, thought, or trial, concluded that the swineherd was the one who had wronged his daughter and determined that he should die. Word reached the swineherd and his friends, who fled into the woods and, being hotly pursued, thence into a marsh. There the outlawed vagrants of the woods ambushed the king. A javelin was hurled into his back. This put an end to the angry life of Lot of Lothian.

The mother and child drifted before the wind into deep waters by the Isle of May in the Firth of Forth and out towards the open sea. Then wind and tide turned suddenly and took the boat upriver, westward, the little boat ploughing the watery breakers, more quickly than if a wind had filled its sails or sturdy sailors plied the oars. The fish followed her little craft in shoals, like a halo of protection. It is told that fish never returned to Aberlady Bay from that day.

All day and night mother and unborn child were on the sea, but when the gleams of morning woke her, the fragile craft was near a shore. She paddled hard, hands scooping the water, and pulled herself ashore in the first sharp pangs of labour. By some brushwood she lay down, beside the cold ashes of a shepherd's fire she prayed for warmth. From the sea came a little puff of breeze. Out of the ashes flew a red star, another, and a whisper of flame. She threw on brushwood, twigs, sticks, logs and was warm in the glowing fire and first flame of the sun. There and then the child was born, and let out a sturdy cry.

She laughed and called it *Kentigern* 'first lord' in her Celtic tongue.

As she huddled, the day stretching before her, some shepherds came by, those whose fire it had been, and found her softly weeping, the new-born baby in her arms. The shepherds took pity on her, banked up the fire, and brought her food and drink.

Others rushed to take the news to the blessed Serf who hearing it said, 'O that such a thing were true!'

'It is true, Holy Father, you will see!'

The woman and the boy were brought to him. And, the strangest thing: when the old man held the little one, only hours old, he looked into the old man's eyes and smiled. The mouth of the old man was filled with spiritual laugher and his heart with joy.

'*Mochohe, Mochohe,*' (my love, my love) said the priest, 'Blessed art thou that hast come in the name of The Lord.'

There, in Culross, Thenaw and Kentigern lived; the young boy learning from priest and mother the love of bird and fish and beast, and growing things, stories of *The Holy Bible* and the Three-in-One God. This is the beginning of the story of the saint, Kentigern.

The Robin

FROM THE WISE TEACHINGS and loving instruction of Serf, the young Kentigern learned fruitfully, as a tree planted by rivers of flowing water. His listening was as a deep pool, his quickness sharp as the eagle's eye, his memory as a deep well, his tongue strong in argument, his voice in song ever honey-sweet and his heart ready to please. It was no wonder that of all those students in his care, Kentigern stood closest to the heart of Serf. So it was his custom to call him in his own tongue *Munghu*, which in Latin, *Karissimus Amicus*, means 'most beloved'. Little wonder too was in it, that his fellow students hated, resented, envied and slandered him, whispered poisonous threats and plotted.

It was the custom of the good Serf to feed a little dainty robin. This little fellow became quite tame and would eat from the hand of the good man. This dainty companion would, while Serf was at study or at prayer, perch upon his head, his shoulder, or his lap and seemed in the glitter of his bright eye, the soft flutter of his wings and his little trills of song to share with the holy man a trance of prayer, so that the face of Serf would radiate with cheerfulness and his lips delight in accompaniments of spiritual laughter. This faithful little friend, so constant and so thirled to the man of God, awoke, as beauty will at times, resentment in the pupils of God's priest.

So it was that when one day the old man took himself to prayer in the chapel, one of the boys, with little trouble, caught the dainty redbreast bird. Others tried to grab and tear it from his grasp, and in the frenzy to possess the prize one tore the head half from the body so that it hung loose and limp and dead, spilling droplets of blood. A silence of horror fell upon the boys who now knew they would, if discovered in this deed, suffer the severest punishment of strokes by the rowan rod. As one they determined to fasten the blame on Kentigern, called him to where they were, and threw the dead bird at his feet near to the cloister from which Serf would return.

Seeing this little creature, the companion of his beloved master, still and lifeless on the ground, the boy Kentigern stooped and lifted him and made a cradle in one hand. He gently and firmly joined the head to body and pressed upon it the sign of the cross praying that He whose breath is in all creatures would give back to this little one the breath of life. At once the bird revived. At that moment it flew in its accustomed bright and fluttering way to where the old Serf emerged from his chapel of prayer.

And so it was in days to come that this little bird, a sign and seal of the goodness of St Kentigern, flew freely on through time to take its place with the salmon amongst the emblems of Kentigern's dear green place, the city of Glasgow.

The Ring

IN THE TIME OF Kentigern was a queen who had everything a mortal could desire; herself comely and beautiful, treasures and jewels in abundance, a husband devoted and loyal, and a son healthy and strong. Her name was Languoreth, her husband the Celtic King Rhydderch. She had time and leisure to indulge every pleasure in full, yet she wanted more. So it was that her eye and her desire fell on a strong young warrior of the king's court, lithe of limb, fresh as spring, a paragon of physical perfection. Upon him settled her lascivious gaze, and she would not, could not, be content until she possessed him.

It was not hard to press this sturdy young warrior to her service, nor hard was it for her to persuade him to share the royal couch. This first rash act, secret, stolen and forbidden, became obsessive, a blinding passion, repeated and repeated. Imprudently in these coils of love, made hotter by intrigue and secrecy, she gave to her young warrior a jewel-encrusted ring her husband the king had given her in the days when he had wooed her. More imprudently he wore this ring.

The sharp eye of a trusted councillor of the king beheld this ring and swiftly concluded its meaning. This he whispered to the king who could not, would not, give his belief to such a thing until with his own eyes he saw the token on the young warrior's hand. In the king's heart serpents of confusion writhed. Yet he took an iron grip upon this torment in his mind and put on an appearance of calm, showing every courtesy to the warrior and to his queen. Soft words were on his lips and seeming kindness in his acts, for he was biding time. One bright and sunshine day he bade the young fresh warrior be his companion in the hunt.

And so with hounds and flanking beaters, off they set, coming in time under some leafy alders on the banks of the River Clyde. There, in no other company, the king and the warrior rested. And there in dappled sunshine they ate and supped fine wine together from which, drowsily, the young warrior fell peacefully asleep. On his outstretched arm the king could see the ring, his gold and jewelled ring, glitter in the sun. Silently he unsheathed his sword and raised it high, directly above the warrior's naked neck. Just then a white swan lighted on the waters of the river and gave the king a moment's pause. Slowly he lowered and quietly sheathed his sword, leaned down, and gently from the young man's finger took the ring and flung it far out into the river Clyde. He had now more fitting punishment in mind.

He woke the warrior and together they rode back to the castle, the young man unconscious of his loss. Into the palace strode the king. The queen smiling and aglow, came from her bed chamber to greet him in the great hall.

Before all the courtiers he spoke out slow and clear, 'Where is my ring?'

Blood ran from her face, 'Your ring, my lord, is safe, safe in my jewel box.'

'I wish to see it. Bring it to me, here. Now.'

'But my lord.'

'Now . . . here this instant, I wish to see it!' A chill of silence fell on all the company.

With no more words the queen hurried from the hall, despatched a maid-in-waiting to her warrior lover and waited, fretting till the maid returned to say that the warrior had lost it and he knew not where, and valiantly he had fled the court. The queen returned to the silent waiting hall.

'I do not recall where I put it, Sire,' said she. 'I thought it to have been safe in my jewel box.'

Into the frozen air of silence the king thundered, 'Adulteress!' the syllables echoed and re-echoed through the hall and soon were whispered in every nook and corner of the palace. 'You have sinned, secretly in the dark. In public in the light of day will be your disgrace! As shameful as the abhorrence of your crime will be your death!'

'Give me time,' said she, 'a little time.'

It was her fortune that some councillors pled on her behalf and three days the king granted her to trace the ring he knew she could not find. For those three days she was put into a dungeon there to 'remember where she had put the ring'!

In the despair and darkness of her dungeon prison she turned in prayer to God, to the merciful Jesus, pleading His forgiveness, not to judge as she deserved, but to show to her the same in infinite mercy He had once shown to another adulteress caught in the very act of her sin. Deep and long she prayed. In the dark of her prison came the gleam of answer to her mind; to seek the intercession of that Christ-like man, the holy Kentigern. So the queen sent a messenger to look for Kentigern, confessing to that messenger the entire unvarnished tale.

At once the messenger set out to seek the holy man, and as it chanced, or as the grace of providence decreed, he met the blessed Kentigern as he approached the dear green place where then he had his humble cell. Before him the messenger bowed, and even before he spoke Kentigern had raised his hand, for his holy insight had divined the whole affair. He ordered the messenger to go at once with hook and line to the banks of the river Clyde and there to throw a cast far into the stream. With the first fish that he caught he was to return.

This command, with every speed, the messenger obeyed. And from the waters at his first cast he pulled a gleaming salmon. He brought this to the holy man who with his knife cut open the belly of the fish and glittering there, revealed the royal ring.

'Take it to Queen Languoreth,' he said.

In despair at her approaching death by shameful means, the queen knelt huddled in her cell. It was close to that hour on the third day, when Languoreth should be brought before King Rhydderch and the assembled court, that the messenger returned. Clasping the ring within her hand the queen could hardly speak. It was as if from death's dark door the golden light of day streamed in. Here was her golden ring miraculously returned.

The cell was opened and she was conducted into the presence

of the king and councillors. Head bowed she approached the king, fell on her knees and with outstretched hand held out the ring. In the hush of that great hall the king took and turned it in his hand, gazed long and hard, and knew without a doubt it was the selfsame ring that in his courting days he had given Langoureth, the ring that he had thrown far into the deep and rushing waters of the Clyde.

Here was the hand of God, the message: 'to forgive'.

What more to say? All was forgiven: *amor omnia vincit,* 'love conquers all'. And the fish, the redemptive salmon, swam into the coat of arms of Kentigern's dear green place, Glasgow, to join the little robin there.

Merlin is Baptised

IT IS TOLD HOW the blessed Kentigern twice met Merlin the Wizard.

Kentigern would take himself into deserted places amongst the giant trees of the forest, Goddeu, now known as Ettrick. There he found solitude, peace and prayer. It is also told that Merlin the Wizard after the internecine war of Briton against Briton, pagan against Christian, after the Battle of Arfderydd at Caerlaverock, fled, mad, deranged, haunted, into this same forest of Ettrick. One day the blessed Kentigern, alone in the thicket of the wilderness, was earnestly praying when a madman, naked, hairy, came upon him staring, mumbling, like some lost demented thing.

The holy man rose and spoke to him, 'In the name of the Father, the Son and the Holy Spirit, speak to me! Who are you who wanders this wild place and keeps the company of beasts? Are you a Christian, man?'

'I am Merlin, once the Bard of Vortigern, wizard to Arthur of Briton, arch druid at the court of King Gwenddolau.

> It was I Merlin, who by my
> powers of magic and of oratory
> inflamed the battle lust in the army of
> Gwenddolau, follower of the ancient
> gods you call pagan. Against the Christian
> Urien we fought, the one they call the
> Golden King of Rheged. And there at
> Arfderdydd, at Caerlaverock,
> Gwenddolau died. The rivers Tweed and
> Ettrick, where they meet ran blood,
> the death blood of the ancient
> gods and all these mighty men.
> From that slaughter field I ran into these
> woods, the voice of gods, demons, in my
> head speaking, "Merlin, you are the

cause of these rivers of blood and
you alone shall penance do,
given to the Dark One, savage and alone,
you will live amongst the
beasts until the very time you die. And
yours shall be the threefold death."

I gazed into the air. Bright light flashed like lances of fire and
gleaming javelins, as if to pierce and torture me. Through thorns and
trackless thickets then I ran, in places only the birds and beasts live.'
    Then this wild man stared like a hunted thing into the skies.
And Kentigern was moved with pity. Tears ran down his face. He
fell upon the earth and prayed,

Lord Jesus, see this most
wretched of wretched men,
cast out to live naked like a
beast among the beasts and
creatures of the wilderness,
take pity, pity him, our brother in
form, flesh, and blood like ourselves ,
who will die in nakedness and
hunger and alone. Take pity,
pity him, Lord Jesus.

And then said Kentigern, 'I dare not either give it to you nor forbid it
you. But there . . . ' he broke bread and placed it on the ground.
'There is the saving victim, laid upon the table of the Lord, approach
it if you will in humbleness and Christ will take you in.'
    And the wild man washed himself in the rivers Tweed and
Ettrick, where they met, approached the altar and kneeling took
the bread, and raised at once his hands and eyes and voice to the
skies in one great shout, 'It is done, Amen!' Then turning to the
holy man he said, 'If this day is the day I die the threefold death,

I prophesy in this same year shall
die the noblest of the nobility, the greatest
King of Britons and the most holy bishop.

The holy bishop laughed, 'My brother, something of your madness
holds you still and of your pagan ways. Go in peace, God be with you.'

And Merlin sprang like a wild goat into the trackless thickets
of the forest, and on that same day, to gather food, he took some
fish set aside by fishermen. They came upon him and on the banks
above the Tweed, a place called Drumelzier, in fury stoned him and
down he fell upon some fish trap spikes. And thus impaled, his body
folded over, went under the water, and he drowned – thus fulfilled
his prophesy and of the threefold death he died.

And of Merlin it was said:

> *Sudeque perfossus, lapide percussus, et unda*
> *Haec tria Merlinum fertur inire necem*
> (Pierced by spear, struck by stones and in water
> By these three Merlin was carried to death.)

And in the same year, The Year of Our Lord 612, as he said so it was:
the blessed Kentigern gave his soul back to God and his spirit
passed into the starry skies.

Brìde Bhìth

A LONG LONG TIME AGO a prince of Ireland, Dugall Donn, was accused of having wronged a woman of noble birth. She bore a child and said that it was Dugall's. Her word was strong in the court of the high king. And so Dugall was sent from Ireland in a small coracle of skins with the baby girl, left to the mercy of wind and rain and storm. But the hand of destiny was upon them, washing their little craft ashore on a beach of Iona.

At once the little baby girl kneeled down, clasped together her fat pink baby hands and sang out in the language of the Gael:

> Chan eil annam ach pàisd, ach cuirear
> m'fhalluinn air Ard righ an t'Saoghail.
> (I am but a little child but my mantle shall be
> laid upon the King of All the World.)

Dugall was amazed that the little one had survived, and more so, to hear her speak in the language of the island Gael. While they lay recovering on the shore, a druid came and welcomed them to the island of Iona. Dugall told the druid that he was a prince of Ireland cast from his land and his people, and falsely accused by a woman of noble birth, of fathering this child.

The druid said, 'Let these thoughts whisper away into the wind. Forget times past. Take this child as your daughter. Make your home here in Iona and let your new name be "Dubthach". 'He led them to a little dwelling by the sea. Dugall the prince of Ireland became Dubthach the farmer of Iona. And the druid said,

> This child will be like no child on earth, let her
> teachers be the wind and the stars, the moon and the sun
> the sea and the birds, leave her much alone
> and let her roam free on the island.

The druid named her 'Brìde'. So it was that Dubthach and his daughter Brìde lived peacefully on Iona.

But Brìde had her own wilful ways and whatever they harvested of fish or of meal she always gave half away. Of every jug of milk she always gave half, though little enough they had for themselves. Brìde, on the morning of her sixteenth birthday, walked up the crest of the hill of Dùn, I at the back of their little farm, to the well of eternal youth to wash her hands and her face in the water. As she climbed she saw the druid dressed in white standing at the top of the hill in prayer, greeting the sunrise.

He hailed and he welcomed Brìde putting upon her a blessing:

> Rise today through the strength of heaven
> light of sun, radiance of moon
> splendour of fire, speed of lightning
> swiftness of wind, depth of sea
> stability of earth, firmness of rock.

While she washed herself in the well of eternal youth she saw reflected in the water a face. Not her own, a beautiful face, gentle and calm. She looked around but no one was there. The memory of this face she kept always in her heart. As she walked one day across the machair toward her father's house she heard a bird singing, sweet beautiful singing. She followed the song of the bird, followed it until the bird flew under an arch where the branches of two rowan trees entwined.

Under this arch she followed and when she looked around to find the bird, it was gone. The sky above was cloudless blue. She looked for the green soft hillsides of Iona and the cool blue sea, but they too were no more. She looked for the thin blue spiral of peat smoke from her father's house, but of smoke or of house nothing was to be seen. She found herself standing instead on sand, hot sand, the sand of the desert, the sun beating down on her face. Across this desert she walked and saw, by and by, a little settlement, and her father's house, which she discovered to be an inn.

She entered and the keeper of the inn said, 'Brìde, it is now three weeks since we have had this drought. There is no drop of water left. Even the cows are dry. I must leave to fetch water and will be gone three days.' He left Brìde in charge of the inn with a bannock and a last stoup of water for her own use. 'Give food or drink to no one. Admit no guest under the roof. If you are careful there will be enough for you until I return.'

Night drew in bitter cold, frosty and starlit. Late in the evening came a knocking at the door. Two strangers stood on the threshold, a man and a woman. That they were hungry, foot weary and thirsty was clear. Old, with thick brown hair and grey of beard, was the man. Young and beautiful the woman, oval her face, gentle her eyes, long and shiny her dark hair. Brìde could see by every sign that the woman was near to delivering a child. The sickness of life was upon her.

As if from a distant dream, as if through still water, Brìde recognized the woman's face, the woman's beautiful face. The man asked for water, food and shelter for the night. She dared not admit them against her master's commands.

And the woman said, 'Brìde, do you not remember me? Will you not let us in?'

And Brìde said, 'I remember you. Wait here.' And she ran in, and there in the doorway gave them her own bannock and the stoup of water.

'I cannot go against my master's commands, you can shelter there in the stable,' she said. 'It is all I can offer,' and she led them to the stable.

When Brìde returned into the inn in the darkening of the night, what was more strange for her to see than that the bannock was whole and the stoup of water once more full in the place where it had been. She did not know under the land of all the world what to think. Here was the food and the water she herself had given them and seen them take, without a bit or a drop now lacking in them. When she recovered herself she went out and saw blazing above the stable door a brilliant golden light, a star!

She came into the stable in time to aid the young woman in her labour, to receive the Baby into her arms and to cover Him with her mantle. For the young woman was Mary, the man, Joseph. From the tips of the fingers of Brìde fell three drops of the water of blessing from the well of eternal youth onto the head of the Baby Jesus. And then from the house she fetched a bucket with fire in it, to warm the cold stable. While she was tending mother and child the flame almost died out.

> The robin noticed and flew down to
> fan it from above with his wings.
> So intent was he on this that the
> kindling flame burnt his breast.
> Mary saw this, thanked and blessed
> him, and the feathers grew again
> red for remembrance.

When the infant in the morning began to cry, the little wren flew down to sing to Him, and the Baby touched the little bird's tail. From that time, Jenny Wren has held her tail high with pride.

When the master returned home with their donkey laden with water, he heard the murmuring music of a stream flowing past the house, and saw above the stable door the light of a bright star. Birds were singing and flowers were bursting to bloom, as if springtime had come to the wide world. By these signs he knew the King of the World was born. Mary and Joseph and the little One of the World stayed with them until it was their time to go.

Brìde was walking one day in the desert when she heard again the song of a bird as from a dream. She followed the bird and its song, followed it through the desert until she came to a place where two trees enfolded into an archway. Under this archway she followed the bird. And as if through a watery dream she found herself again with the sweet green grass of Iona lapping her ankles, the fresh salt scent of the sea in her nostrils, and saw there in the distance the spiral of thin peat smoke from her father's cottage. She was home, Brìde Bhìth, Brigid of the Isles, the handmaid of Mary.

The Birth of Colum Cille

WHEN ALL THINGS ALIVE had whispering voices, and the veil between this world and the otherworld was thin, the holy ones through trance and dream could see far into years to come. In that bright dawn many tongues foretold the coming of a mighty man whose words and deeds, like ocean waves crashing against rocky coasts, would break upon the shore of Erin and of Alba and upon lands and ages yet unborn. This man was Crimthann, the fox of battle, Colum Cille, Dove of the Church.

Legend tells that two hundred years before his birth the aged priest Mochta of Wouth prophesied one would come: 'Erin he will set alight, his death leave Alba drenched in tears, Colum Cille will be his name.'

The holy Brigit dreamed:

> In the North will grow a sapling into a mighty tree,
> its branches reaching over Erin, Alba and the western world.

Not alone was it the saints and patriarchs that foretold of this man of fire, but druids too, and that skilled hunter-warrior of the Fianna, its legendary leader Finn mac Cumhaill.

With one of his favourite hounds Bran, whose death was to bring weeping to his eyes, Finn was tracking a fleet white deer. At the river of Senglenn, close on its quarry, suddenly Bran ceased the chase, a thing of wonder for never before but once at the hunt of the enchanted Saba had Bran not fastened teeth and brought down the prey. Seeking reason for this riddle of the hunt Finn put his thumb against his gifted tooth of wisdom, and in that trance discerned in future time a man whose god was three, a victor over the minds of people in the Celtic kingdoms of Erin and Alba. It was in token of this that Bran would not cross that river to pursue the deer.

Many others there were in that age of clear-seeing who foretold the birth of Colum Cille. Of no blood more noble was he to be born, his father Fedlimid descended from Niall Noígiallach (of the

Nine Hostages), high king of Ireland, his mother Eithne descended from Cathair Mór, king of Leinster.

While Eithne yet carried within her this child marked out by these fiery foretellings, a little cloud of sleep came on her and she dreamed a riddling dream. From a golden mist, out of the mouth of morning, she held in her arms a cloak with the fragrance and colours of every flower and fruit and sweet-scented thing. Over mountains and seas spread this cloak of colours. Then came a man and seized it from out her arms so that where he had taken it she could in no way see, and woke and wept.

Near the time her child was to come through the door of birth a holy man, Fergna came to visit her and was welcomed by the unborn child. It was said: 'he stretched his thumb out from his mother's womb, a thing never heard of before. No nor since.'

When the pains of birth were on her, into a lonely glen by a small stream went Eithne. The winter gold sun sank over the mountains and the silver moon rose. It was on Thursday, the seventh day of December in the year 520 AD that Colum Cille was born. The place was Rath Cnó in Gartan in the north of Ireland. His birth bed was a cold flagstone.

In that place, and alone, Eithne bore this child whose later Christian name, Colum Cille 'the Dove', would carry messages across the world. When the old priest Cruithnechan put water to the baby's head it was not Colum Cille he named him but Crimthann, that is, the Fox, 'wily one' in the tongue of the Gael. There in the gloaming half light where night meets day he took his first breath. On such a pillow of stone would he take his last.

Wily One

THE RED FOX made his silent way out of the throat of night towards his prey. In the dusky chapel Crimthann stalked the beauty of words, manuscripts of the Holy Scriptures, precious to him as the blood of life itself. From these words shone the poetry of God.

Fortune favoured Crimthann; for had his spiritual master the holy monk Finnias of Moville brought over the swelling seas from Rome not only a Psalter of the Mosaic Law, but also the gospels themselves, translated by the sainted Jerome? This precious manuscript Finnias guarded as if it were his heart. In his chapel safely it lay and access to it, as a mighty act of love, he gave to one of his talented and favourite pupils, Colum Cille (the dove of the church), Crimthann (the fox). Read it he might, but to copy it he was forbidden. It was the Dove of the Church who in candle glow read these words, as if they were the light of love, the breath of life. It was Crimthann, the red fox of Erin that crept in secretly by night to copy them and have them for his own.

Night after night, the vespers over, they as one together entered the chapel, the Christian Dove of the Church, the pagan Pictish Fox, one reading, one writing. The thief, the holy monk caught in a rapture out of time or place.

From a troubled dream old Finnias awoke. A thief was plundering his flock of sheep. In this dream the old man was a shepherd boy on the hills of Galilee, and out of the gloom of night came wolves savaging his flock of sheep. Finnias called upon a young novice that attended him and sent him to the chapel to fetch his manuscript so that he might find some rest and comfort in the words of God.

When the young novice quietly opened the chapel door Colum Cille in a total trance was fixed upon his task like a limpet to a rock. From crane's quill in his hand flowed the last words of the fourth gospel: 'If all the wonders done by Jesus were recorded, not the world itself could contain the books that should be written.'

Out from the night stole the red fox and the hen gave one

fluttering squawk as his teeth fastened on her neck. Columba leaped up like a warrior from sleep, bristling, wary, ready and saw the wide eyes and wide mouth of the novice boy, frightened, awed at what he had discovered, this thief of holy writ, this favourite fallen like brightest Lucifer from grace.

'Keep your tongue still!' said Colum Cille and jabbed the quill into the boy's cheek so that from it ran a tear of blood. The boy flew from the chapel and garbled to the kneeling Finnias what he had found. Finnias heard as one struck with wounds, pain and anger and sorrow took tears to his eyes, the blood from his face.

White as bone he came into the chapel where Colum Cille waited. Before him, illumined by candle glow lay the two manuscripts, the ink of the last sentence of the copy he had made not yet dry. Quietly the old man spoke, his voice a keen blade.

'Without permission, and in deceit, you have made this copy and so rightfully, the son of my book, it is mine.'

In matching measure Colum Cille replied, 'As a judgement on that I will seek the ruling of Diarmait high king of Ireland. His justice is good: Let his words settle the matter.' Each sure of the judgement following in his own favour they journeyed together at the sunrise of that morning to Tara of the kings, to the stronghold of Diarmait mac Cerbaill, high king of Ireland.

'Speak, Finnias,' said the king.

'Under my roof of hospitality Colum Cille copied my book secretly, and I say the copy of my book is mine.'

"Colum Cille, what do you say?'

'I say that none, not I nor any other should be hindered from copying the holy words, for to everyone they should belong. No profit comes to me from this labour but riches to all who may know the words. No harm is on Finnias nor on his book and so I say the copy I have made is mine.'

'According to the ancient law of the brehon,' said Diarmait, 'I say to every cow its little cow, its calf: and for that reason, Colum Cille, the judgement is for Finnias. The book you copied is from Finnias and so belongs to him.'

A flame of warrior rage blazed in the blood of Colum Cille. 'It is a false judgement. You will pay.' And his anger glowed red in the embers. These embers soon would blaze.

At this time Diarmait the high king was in dispute with Eógan king of Connacht, a friend of Colum Cille. Diarmait held hostage Cumain, the son of Eógan of Connacht. As befitted the son of a king, Cumain was treated well. He was tall, strong and quick of temper. On an afternoon he was playing in a hurling match and in the game he and Connacht's steward tangled sticks. The steward made some slighting words and Cumain smote him with his stick on the brow with such a blow as killed him instantly. Fleet of foot young Cumain fled and found sanctuary in the chapel of Colum Cille.

From that holy place, when the grey blackness of night had fallen, four men of Diarmait dragged him out and blow for blow broke in his skull bones so that in the orange red path of morning outside the chapel he lay dead. The colour of the sun rising in the mist was the rage that rose in the breast of Colum Cille when his eyes fell on the head of Cumain. That rage would burn a fire through the glens of all the western world. He would go at once to arouse his kinsmen the Uí Néills to avenge the sacrilege, the breach of holy sanctuary, and the words that stabbed and rumbled over in his mind: 'to each cow his calf.'

'A threefold death fall on Diarmait,' he vowed, an echo of the Celtic curse of old that simmered in his blood. Warned that Diarmait's forces waited him in ambush, Colum Cille through the hilly lands of Howth took his way on foot, the poet speaking in him as he went to the stronghold of his kinsmen the Uí Néill chieftains, Cenél Conaill and Cenél Eógain:

> Alone I am upon the mountain
> King of Heaven, smooth my way.
> No more fear as in me now than if
> six thousand were my shield.
> For my druid is Christ, Great Abbot,
> Father, Son and Holy Spirit.

He made his way to the stronghold of his kinsmen the Uí Néill chieftains, Cenél Conaill and Cenél Eógain. In their ears his word was strong for they had cause of their own to settle with Diarmait. To avenge the death of his son, Cumain, King Eógan brought his warriors and together over green Erin to Cúl Dremne the armies made their march.

In Colum Cille the voices of his warrior ancestors, Niall of the Nine Hostages, Conn of the Hundred Battles, cried out: 'You have been slighted, dishonoured. A man lives after his life, but not after his honour.'

The old gods and the new one were at war in his breast. The battle fury of Cúchulainn, the vengeful god of the Old Testament, kept out of his ear the voice of that God whose words were love. Vengeance for wrongs put memories of the druid priests, their spells and their curses before battle, into the front of his mind. The new god stayed his hand from sword and spear but metal flashed and glinted in his morning prayer. It was no dove of peace but hunting fox and swooping eagle ruled.

On the hill-top sat Colum Cille, behind the gathered host of his kinsmen, the northern Uí Néills and the forces of the Connacht king, come to avenge the death of Cumain, dragged from holy sanctuary. On a milk-white steed sat this divided man, Crimthann, the Fox and Colum Cille, Dove of the Church.

'Father, Greatest Druid,' he prayed as the mist of morning thinned in the drying sun, and across the valley he could discern the mighty army gathered by all Ireland's high king, Diarmait.

> Let our men fall like wolves
> upon these sheep and put
> fear into the men of Diarmait
> and into our warriors, the battle fury.
> For victory on this day I will
> give my life.

His mighty voice rang out an ancient war cry so thunderous that the men of Diarmait heard it. Like the war horn of the Fianna it fell, a spear shower upon their hearts.

At the day's darkening three thousand men lay dead, the green valley and the river red with blood, and total victory was with the Uí Néill and Connacht. A little body only of men were lost to them that day but Colum Cille would pay with his every day the cost of that great victory.

And the name of that place was Cúl Dremne and the place where Colum Cille stood while battle raged got the name *Suidhe Colum Cille* 'the seat of Colum Cille', though some have said that he himself carried sword, took a wound in that battle and carried the livid scar of it for all his days. It is well known that in his side he bore a jagged scar.

The Dream

The blood of three thousand is on
you, Colum Cille, from these men, by
your vengefulness and in the name of
the God of love
you have torn the sweet breath of life,
young men of Erin.
Widows and mothers keen their sorrow
the little rivers weep for the children of Erin.
The wind laments and from the trees leaves fall like tears.
On the throne of your heart sat pride and this is your making.
Your feet are not worthy to tread this land nor
you to have sweet concourse with the
men and women and children of Erin,
not with the hounds or creatures of the forest.
Not worthy are you to taste the honey sweet fruits
nor fish nor fowl nor food nor drink of this green land.
Not the water of the holy well will
sain the blood that stains your hand.
To the raven cold coast of Alba go,
never to return and to make some penance for
your deeds, bring three times three thousand souls from that
land of Picts and pagan gods into the bosom of
the God of Love.

IN A SHIVERING COLD Colum Cille awoke from this dream, where
it seemed from a lofty and craggy sea girt rock a mighty figure
stood wreathed in cloudy mist, his voice like thunderous waves
upon a shore. Through that hazy air his eye-gaze pierced like spear
thrusts upon the kneeling Colum Cille. Behind this figure in a glow
of white, as of a wind-blown flame, a woman beckoned, beckoned
and faded in the brightening air. Then both were gone but the
shadows in his mind remained and echoes, echoes of that giant's

words like branding irons upon his heart. This dream was prophecy for at the conclave of holy men at Teilte, abbots, monks and scholars, was the edict passed that banished Colum Cille from his native Erin, the conditions as those spoken in his terrible dream.

In a little stream that flowed into Lough Foyle Colum Cille kneeled down, cupped his hands with the cool fresh water, and drank. Once more he filled his hands and splashed his face so that the water fell and washed away the salty tear drops. On both sides of Lough Foyle they stood when they saw that Colum Cille in truth was leaving them, kinsmen and countrymen, the house of Conall and Eógan Uí Néill, monks, poets, children, friends. His boat pushed off into the water of the Lough and after him they raised an outcry and lament so that he scarce could listen to that sound. The poet in him spoke out.

> The cry of lamentation of the people of Derry of
> my kinsmen Eógan and Conall breaks
> four quarters of the heart within me.
> Not till my death
> will the sound leave my ears.
> Like resistless waves of the sea
> will it return in the tide of days.
> No night will pass without my tears.
> Hard it is this exile from the Gaels
> I love, the strong sweet kin of Erin.
> Hard it is to breathe more.

Amongst his companions in the boat was the holy Oran. 'Put your thoughts and strength to the task that is your gift from God,' he said. 'Do not look backwards. Ahead is our great voyage.'

'It is good you say these words, my friend, and yet to leave is like the soul taken from the body, the breath taken out, to part from birth land and kin to be for ever a pilgrim wanderer.'

'Aye. For God!' said Oran.

Screaming and screeching on both sides of the boat seagulls and birds of Lough Foyle followed the exiles and then as the curach came into the open sea of white-topped waves they wheeled and left. Colum Cille's back was to Ireland when the boat came into the blue green turmoil of the Corrievreckan whirlpool.

It was the first of many struggles for the body, heart and spirit of Colum Cille and for the monks he took with him to the shores of Alba. On the foam-flecked sea, bold across the sea's ridge, riding the surge of the wave-torrent it was not to the holy island of Iona that the curach of Colum Cille came, but to the beach of Colonsay.

Then said Oran from a high rock on the shore, 'I yet can see green Erin.'

'Then on!' said Colum Cille. So on they voyaged. Some say it was long the search and many the stopping places till to the blessed isle they came, that holy jewel whose sparkle would radiate around the earth, to Iona, the burial ground of many kings.

Ancestral voices of the druid times and the power in their ancient rites still spoke in the mind of Colum Cille and standing on the shore, gazing round he said,

It is good our roots should go beneath the earth and
one who gives his life to be buried here, a
willing sacrifice will forthwith be alive
among the blessed dead in the
holy presence of our God.

It was that same holy companion Oran who stepped forward after the manner of old druid rites and offered himself for sacrifice to consecrate that place.

The manner of Oran's dying no legend for certain tells, but some have said it was the threefold death he died, that was the ritual custom of the druid Celtic priests. But others say he was buried alive.

Three nights and days he was interred and at the sun setting of the third the earth was lifted from his body by order of Colum Cille, and all who stood there were amazed for Oran breathed, opened his eyes and spoke,

'The heav'n is not as they averring claim
nor is the hell as they asserting say,
the good is not for ever bliss the same
the bad is not a misery for aye.'

Into the hearts of every monk there fell an awe of silence. From out this silence beside the grave Colum Cille at once in wisdom the answer gave,

'Let earth once more on Oran's body fall
before confusions from his words fly free
and into chaos plunges all
for darkly through a glass on earth
it is ordained for men to see.'

And so it was. What is known and told, beneath the clay they buried Oran. From that time the place has the name *Reilig Oran* 'the graveyard of Oran'.

Flyting for Souls

NOT ALONE WAS Colum Cille in taking the message of the Christ God to the Pictish people of Caledonia. The Pictish Irish monk Moluag made his centre for a time Shian on the tip of Benderloch. In his sea path from Iona, Colum Cille came to this district named for the son of fox. There Moluag welcomed his countryman from Erin.

On a soft morning when the sea was silken down by the shore, these two men of God were in friendly talk until the good Moluag remarked, 'I go tomorrow to that island of Lismore now in mist, to bring its people into the sunshine of the God of Love.'

'For that purpose came I here,' said Colum Cille, 'and tomorrow mean to set out.'

'This is my task,' said Moluag, 'therefore have I made this place my cell. The island is closest to where my work has been. This island is mine for God.'

'No island is yours in this land more than mine. I go at sunrise,' said Colum Cille rising.

'That is my intention,' said Moluag also rising and gazing towards the misty island of Lismore as a warrior preparing for battle.

'So be it,' said Colum Cille, 'together in our separate crafts we will set sail and that man whose flesh and blood is first upon the shore, his shall be the island.'

As the red sun rose out of the mouth of morning, glinting russet on the rocky shore, the two coracles of skin slipped into the water, in one Colum Cille, Moluag in the other. The monks and followers of these holy adversaries crowded the shore to witness this race, whose stakes were human souls for God. Colum Cille was confident, wave-hardened, his seamanship tried and victorious in the swirling vortex of the Corrievreckan whirlpool, he who had withstood the contrary winds of Devil curses, skilled in sail and oar, his strong heart sang for he was at ease. Moluag was in the waters he knew well, the tides and eddies, currents and flows. Here he had drawn fish, outfaced the sea dragons, made companions of the dolphins, otters, whales, and heard the seafolk frolic and sing. His heart was strong in the chase as a fleet hound for deer on the high hill. As Lismore drew near, each as warriors in spear clash smote the waters, prow for prow, so that it seemed a riddle who might first have beached his craft till at the last by strength of arm Colum Cille pulled ahead his little boat.

Seeing this, Moluag drew from his belt a keen blade knife and with one swift cut he sliced the top from off his little finger, flung it to the land and laughing loud, held up his blooded hand in victory, with it made a sweeping cross and said, 'My flesh and blood have first possession of the island and I bless it and its people in the name of the all powerful Lord!' Colum Cille seeing his brother monk had outwitted him began to call down curses on Moluag's occupation of the island.

'May the alder be your firewood!' he shouted.

'And the Lord make it to burn sweetly!' replied Moluag.

'May your pathways be jagged ridges,' said Colum Cille.

'And the Lord smooth them to my feet,' said Moluag.

'May the cold mist out of the mouth of morning keep your eyes from seeing.'

'And the bright Son of God break through to clear my seeing.'

Many more were the flytings they fired like croaking rooks through the bright air until at last, as two grey seals barked at one another on the rocks in mockery, the mouths of each monk filled with laughter. Yet in the end it was Colum Cille whose cross rose on Lismore. For Moluag, great wanderer, made pilgrimages across Alba following the track of St Ninian to the east and died at Rosemarkie, much lamented.

Dair and Lugne

DAIR HAD ALWAYS FELT free as a bird on the island. It was the island of her birth, the island of her heart. She loved to sit upon the little hill above the croft that was her home, to sit and gaze out to sea, the sea like a water meadow stretching into the blue distance, the colours gleaming and fading into the far horizon. Below her the wind-tossed horses of the waves pranced ashore. Above, high in the puffy blue, sang larks, and before her sea birds swooped and floated like a melody in the air. Now as she sat there she remembered that day three years ago, the summer day, hot and dry, when she had looked down and there was Lugne the Hunchback dragging his boat from the water, lifting his catch from the sea.

And at the shore the island children laughed at him, mocked and mimicked him, called him names, made his hunchback shape ugly as a troll. They feared him, threw stones at him. As he hirpled away from them bearing his burden of fish, set awry on the great hump on his back, he looked pained and anguished and lonely.

Dair had been to the well for water. And when she saw this struggling lonely man hirpling with his burden along the shore her heart filled with pity. She ran to him, raised her pitcher to his lips. He drank the cool water of the well and looked at her with large dark, thankful eyes. After the shouting, the stones, the ugly names, in the heat of the day Lugne never forgot this little act of kindness. In his heart he kept the picture of this tender girl coming to him, bringing him fresh cool water from the well.

The next summer was wet, windy, full of gales from the west. The crops were ruined and a fierce winter fastened a grip on the island. The people went hungry and without food, they died. It was then in the winter bareness that Lugne came to the door of Dair's home and left salted fish, grain he had stored, fuel for the fire. And so they lived through the bare winter. And one day when Spring smiled once more on the island Dair's father met Lugne by the shore.

'Lugne, you kept the breath in us all this winter,' he said. 'How can I ever repay you?'

Out of the lonely yearning of Lugne's heart came his answer: 'There is a way. I would like to marry Dair.'

'No, no, no, no!' said Dair. 'I cannot marry him. He is ugly, ugly! I could not look on him.'

'Dair,' said her father gently, 'we owe him our lives. But for Lugne, your brothers and sisters would be under the earth. How can we ever repay that? Dair, I would give him anything I own for saving our family, for keeping us alive.' Suddenly the island seemed without charm, a prison, the gulls mocking demons in the sky, the sea cruel and dark.

At last she said, 'Father, for what he has done I will marry him, but I cannot love him.'

'So be it,' said her father. 'I ask no more.'

And so it was. They married in a tiny stone oratory down by the shore. And she cooked for Lugne, made and mended clothes, cleaned the house, but she could not love him. And Lugne the Hunchback knew this, knew she could not love him, could not look on him with any pleasure. And he was sad in the sadness of his lonely crumpled prison. He had little joy any more in his work. And with the hump on his back he carried a hump of sadness in his heart.

One of Lugne's tasks was as ferryman.

It was a bright day of summer and Dair was sitting on the hill she had loved. Looking down on the sea she saw Lugne's strong arms row the boat towards the shore. And it seemed to her that there was a glow about the boat, about the figure settling in the prow, a golden glow. Lugne's passenger was Colum Cille, Columba, the Dove of the Church. She ran down the hill to their little house and while Lugne beached and secured the boat she watched Columba stride up the beach.

The man of God came straight to where she stood at the door of their little stone house. He took her small hands into his strong gnarled ones.

'You are the wife of Lugne are you not?' She nodded. 'He spoke of you in the boat.'

'Yes,' she said, 'I am his wife, but I cannot love him!' Columba looked at her gently, gently. 'I look after his needs, I sew for him, mend for him, clean for him, cook for him, but I cannot love him. I had rather cross the sea and join a household of maidens. I believe there are such who live their lives for God and do not marry. I had rather go to such an island!'

'Do you believe,' said Colum Cille, 'that God is love?'

'Yes,' said Dair.

'And that with the love of God, all things are possible?' Looking into the eye of this man Dair could believe it.

'Yes,' she said.

'Then let us all, each in our separate place of prayer, ask God to bring love where it is not. Will you do this?'

'I will try to pray,' said Dair. She did not believe she could come to love Lugne.

That night Lugne went to the little stone oratory to pray. Colum Cille walked by the seashore in prayer under the bright glow of the moon. Dair sat on a stool by the window and heard the endless sobbing of the sea. She tried to pray but always, like a ghostly troll, the face of Lugne forlorn, piteous, ugly, came before her to accuse her loveless, loveless heart. At last, in a torment, she could bear it no longer. Dark clouds scurried over the moon throwing flickering shadows across the island. She shivered, put on her shawl and went outside.

The moon came from a cloud clear and bright, and cast the jagged shadow of a thorn tree on the ground. Suddenly it took the shape of a monstrous prowling beast grotesque and horrible, its claws outstretched to savage her. In terror she shrank against the walls of the house and turned to face the beast. There stood Lugne his large dark eyes abrim with such a look of love that suddenly she remembered him as on that summer day when she had brought him water from the well. She threw her arms around his neck, his strong frame shivering. She felt his huge strength and his terrible weakness.

'Lugne, come in,' she said, 'and I will keep you warm.'

When the sun shone out of the mouth of the morning Columba came from the seashore to where they sat at the fire. Together they ate breakfast and then Lugne went to make ready the boat.

'Do you still wish,' said Colum Cille, 'to join the household of the island of women?'

She laughed. 'No, no, no,' she said, 'the island is too beautiful, too beautiful to leave.'

And now she sat once more on her beautiful hill. Below her, like a blue meadow, the sparkling sea, above the larks sang in the puffy clouds. And from there Dair watched her husband Lugne with strong arms ferry the Dove of Peace on his journey. And the boat seemed doubly aglow.

Little Red Squirrel

COLUM CILLE, Dove of the Church, Columba of Iona, was down-hearted. The great enterprise seemed to have faltered, his patience tried to breaking point. The Pictish tribes were reverting to the old ways, to their pagan gods.

'God, give me a sign, some sign that I should go on,' he prayed.

In a little coracle Columba crossed from Iona to Mull, and in this dejected state of mind, near despair, he was walking in the woods when he came to a clearing. There by the lochside was a little red squirrel. It was dipping its tail in the loch and splish splashing drops of water onto the shore.

'What are you doing?' asked Colum Cille, puzzled by this strange activity.

'I'm emptying the loch,' said the squirrel.

Columba laughed and said kindly enough, 'You will never empty the loch like that, not in the whole of your lifetime. Never.'

The little bright eyes blinked and then the squirrel nodded and said, 'I suppose you are right. Thank you.' And so Columba turned and was walking away when, splish, splash, he heard again and turned and saw his little friend once more dipping its bushy tail in the water and splish, splash onto the shore.

'I told you,' said Columba, 'you will never empty that loch, not in your whole lifetime.'

'You are right', said the little red squirrel, 'but it will make it easier for the ones that come after me.'

The Devil in Skye

ON THE ISLAND OF Skye in times long since, the Vaternish peninsula was a favourite haunt of wolves and their last outpost on the island. One of these gray lupine marauders was a great friend of the Devil and had, at the time of our tale, been about some satanic business for his lordship.

Now it is well known that the Devil's bed is nettles, for when that proud master and his followers were cast from Heaven, where they fell on earth nettles sprang up. They have followed his footsteps ever since, and ever since have been his bed. '*Faran bheil feanntagan bithidh mallachd air an aite sin*' (nettles are a sign of a place accursed), so say the Gaelic folk of the islands.

The proud Devil waking on his stingy bed one morning was black in mood, glowering at the sunny day from under his handsome brow. His demonic minions had informed him that the holy man Colum Cille, the so called Dove of the Church, a favourite of God as he himself long since had been, was on the island, was indeed nearby in Trotternish. The Devil's spirit lightened, a pleasing spark had entered the mind of the father of lies.

With sad and downcast eyes the Devil came before the good Columba. Raising his head from prayer, the holy man beheld a figure pitiful and abject, red-rimmed eyes, and of an appearance so abject as would draw tears from a stone.

Kneeling in this posture of humility and anguish the Devil begged the good man to intercede with the Lord on his behalf, and ask that he might have another plant than nettles. Moved by this piteous plea Colum Cille promised the Devil he would speak to the Lord, and make this request.

When next the good Colum Cille came before the Lord he kept his promise to the Devil. God was surprised by this plea but knowing the goodness of the faithful follower before him He said, 'Because it is you who ask, you whose heart can find compassion even for that dark prince, I will grant your asking. 'Now,' said God, 'in Scotland he is, well, let him have barley. Of that there is enough.'

Columba returned. Before him that king of deceivers stood bowed with downturned mouth and upcast eyes, like a devout and earnest penitent.

'God, in his mercy, has granted you barley.'

On his knees the Devil thanked him but in his black heart he danced like a bride at a wedding. Out of sight down the glen and over the hills he skipped and pranced to Vaternish. There he met his friend the wolf. His gray friend and follower, proudly and at great length, told him how successful had been his devilish mission on his behalf. Meantime, old Satan fidgeted and pranced from hoof to hoof and could not contain his unholy glee. The wolf noticed and remarked upon the unaccustomed cheerfulness of his dark master.

'At last,' said the Devil, 'God has given me another plant.'

'What plant?' said the wolf.

Sudden as thunder from a bruised sky the Devil glowered brimstone, eyes red flames of rage. The wolf cowered.

'You!' said the Devil, 'with all your boastful prattling and talk of what *you* have done, have put it from my mind!' Desperately the wolf sought to make amends.

'Heather, perhaps,' he suggested.

'Fool! Nothing so common!' he hissed.

'Thistles, then?'

'No, not thistles.' He scratched his head so that sparks of naked anger flashed in the air. 'Wait, wait,' he said, 'something useful ...'

And of course, what God gives, no man nor beast can take away and so it was that barley came to belong to the Devil. Now many there are who say that Columba, and even God, made a mistake in giving the Devil barley, since from it he made his own devilish brew and so outwitted them. But others say that this was only a wise and witty way of having the Devil do God's heavenly work by conferring upon humankind *uisge beatha* 'the water of life', whisky, John Barleycorn!

The Black Boar of Celyddon

ON THE ISLAND OF Skye under the shadow of Bruach na Frithe 'the steep bank of the deer forest,' in the great Cuillin mountains, Colum Cille kneeled in prayer. Free and strong and clear flowed the little river from the mountain, flowed Allt an Fhionn Choire, the stream of Finn's corrie.

'As the waters of this stream,' he prayed, 'Lord, give me strength and fluency and clarity to take the Living Water to the very king of Pictland, there to meet at the loch-head of the monster in the Great Glen of Alba.' His young novices at that time were close in pursuit of a great wild boar. Into the clearing by the river where the holy man was praying burst the mighty beast straight in the path of Colum Cille.

With warrior speed of thought and hand the holy man thrust his hazel staff into one glaring eye of this black boar. The beast let out a squeal of pain. In savage boar-rush into the undergrowth of the forest of Celyddon hurtled the wounded beast.

The day was hot. Becuma, slim and dusky dark, struggled from the lochside up the rough stone steps to the house of Broichan, druid to the Pictish king Brude. Becuma was the slave of this wizard. Round her neck was a halter suspending two heavy water pitchers. Her bare feet picked their way up the rough stairway cut through the forest. She was lean and strong and lonely.

'I am as my name,' she was thinking. Bheag thu mhath, 'worth you little' in the Gaelic tongue of the land from which she had been captured. For that green Erin of her childhood she longed and in her solitude wept to be separated from her little sister, Ciara. Where was Ciara, the little brown nut of her heart? Where was she now?

She passed the guards at the entrance gate to the great stone fortress of king Brude and came to the house within the courtyard where lived her master. His magical power was next to that of the king. She feared his words and his blows. On this day Broichan had a visitor.

This was the man of the new god of whom she had heard people in the village talk, the same man upon whom she had heard Broichan lay curses, the man who challenged the gods of the Pictish people. This was Colum Cille, who carried the story of the new god whose son, it was said, the people killed and hanged on a tree. In her heart Becuma pitied this god for had she not seen the terrible tears of her own father when her brother was slain before his eyes.

The thongs of the halter bit deep into her skin and swiftly she set down the pitchers, water spilling from them as she did so. When he saw this, hot words flew from the wizard's tongue and his gaze fell upon rods of birch standing at the wall of the house. The girl, of no more it seemed than fourteen summers, looked up in cold dread and then cast down his eyes.

'Who is this girl and why do you speak to her in this way?' said Colum Cille who had not missed the direction of the wizard's glance.

'She is my slave, mine to do with as I will.'

'You will set her free,' said the holy man. Broichan laughed.

'At whose command shall I set her free? She belongs to me!' Before the door of this magician's house the two men stood, face to face, men of equal size and strength, the Pictish priest and the monk of Iona. Colum Cille looked into the cool grey eyes before him.

'Your breath will not long be in you and your body will be in spasms, if this girl is not free when I leave your lands.' Colum Cille looked down at the trembling slave girl. 'You will find the little brown nut of your heart,' he said. 'Your feet will walk that sweet green land again. You will be free.' Turning once more to the silent Broichan he said, 'The cup will crack and spill out your life! In the path death waits for you.' With that he turned and strode from the stronghold of king Brude in the Great Glen of Scotland. After some days with his little band of monks he made his way to the banks of the river Ness.

Dipping his hand in the waters he pulled out a gleaming white pebble and said to his companions, 'Mark this blessed stone, for in it is the power of healing. From that power many who are sick shall be well, unless it is indeed the Lord's appointed time to take them from this earth.' He paused and stood silent as if listening. 'Broichan is struck, the cup of glass from which he drinks is shattered. He struggles to breathe and death stands by his side. The fear of death is on him. Presently will come two men on horseback, sent from the king to ask our help.'

These words were hardly out when at a gallop came two horses, sweat-flecked, the riders breathless. They slid from their mounts and before the man of God spilled out their tale, told how, at the side of king Brude after a great feast stood Broichan laughing and mocking at a god who was so weak that his own son was hanged from a tree. They told how, as he raised his cup of glass to drink, it shattered in his hand, the liquor like blood splashing his robe and spattering the ground. They told how the blood ran from his face and how he fell upon the ground and lay as if about to die and was now willing to let the slave girl go free. This message they brought by command of the king himself and asked help from the great white wizard Colum Cille.

'Take this stone and these words to king Brude,' said Colum Cille. 'If Broichan upon the oath of his own gods sets free the Irish slave girl put this stone into a water bowl and from it let him drink. His sickness will at once be gone. If he refuses still or breaks his word then in that moment his breath will cease.' Without resting the messengers returned to the stone fort of Brude above the River Nesa, with them two of the followers of Colum Cille.

Broichan, who was the foster son of Brude, lay pale, his breath short and shallow, cold perspiration on his brow. The king was at his side and heard the message of the man of this new god. Within an hour the slave girl was released. The white pebble was dropped into a shallow bowl where to the wonder of those who watched, it floated on the surface like an apple or a nut. The bowl was put to the lips of Broichan who sipped and drank from the healing cup. Colour came to his face, his breath grew deep. He blinked as one awaking to bright sun and was in body once more sound and well.

And yet all that being so and the great wonder in it, Broichan kept still his devotion to the ancient gods.

Becuma, the slave girl returned with the monks to the island of Iona. There, as the swooping, wheeling gulls in the bright air she ran barefoot, heedless and free over the island with songs from her childhood brimming in her heart, flowing through her life. Then one day, from the shore, Colum Cille raised his hand in blessing and she set sail on a little coracle of skins, with two monks to accompany her, on a journey to the soft green glens of Erin.

Colum Cille watched the little craft sail the fair winds until it was a wisp, a speck, an imagining, and it brought a little weeping to his eye that her feet would walk the land he again would never tread. There as he had foretold she met again with tears of joy, her little sister Ciara and true to the prophecy of the holy monk, the stone healed many people, floating wondrously upon the cup of water before the sick drank of it. Yet when it was the appointed time for one to leave this earth the stone would sink in this cup as the life of the sick one too sank into death.

On the day king Brude died the stone could not be found in the place where, until then, it had been carefully kept. No one now knows where it is.

Dark and Light

ALONE IN HIS CELL in the seventy-seventh year of his life, Colum Cille, through the thickening mist of years, saw beckoning like the sun the golden light of that eternal land where, the earthly struggles over, he would rest on the soft breast of peace. He recalled calmly as a drowning man, when the grasp for breath is over, the days of his life. The merry days amongst the poets of Erin, the hours drunk with joy inscribing holy manuscript, the blood strewn field of Cúl Dremne, leaving Erin on the trackless seas, quelling the charging black boar on Skye, the little God-sent squirrel, the ferocity and beauty of the world. He prayed his thanks and asked that this night the door of death would open to take him in. As he raised his eyes his solicitous friend Diarmad stood by the door; Diarmad the anxious, the doubting one, who feared that right and justice never would come.

'Come sit,' said the holy Colum Cille. 'I once had three pets, a fly, a wren, a cat. To them I spoke and they to me. One day my wren ate my fly and that same day my cat ate the wren. I prayed to God:

> Bring back from
> my cat my wren and from
> my wren my fly.

And so He did, and I had them by me until the close of their natural lives. So will it be with men in future times as now. The strong will devour the weaker, take their wealth and goods, give them neither rights nor justice, Diarmad. Foreign powers will rule over them until in themselves justice and right have sway. Then once more will they have the keeping of their own lands. Even so will it be in my own birth land of Erin and in lands beyond. That is the story of my pets. Be cheerful, Diarmad. Take me to see the corn store of the monks.'

As they walked Colum Cille said, 'Pray loud, long and loud enough, good Diarmad, and God's ears will hear. Do you not recall when the mighty gates of the Pictish King Brude were closed against us and I prayed loud, loud and long?'

'Like thunder overhead,' said Diarmad.

'I think I frightened the gates open, or frightened those within to open them.' The old man's laughter broke from him like a gushing well. 'That old Brude,' he continued, 'at last, at least, was half a Christian man. Never did he oppose me but with Broichan the pagan gods still ruled.' Sparks of the warrior lit his face in recollecting those dangerous days.

They came to the monk's hay yard, their grain store, and there were gathered two great heaps of corn. A mist of thanks was in the eyes of Colum Cille. He cared like a mother for his monks, thanking God that as his last hour neared, the corn store was full so that a long winter would not put the pains of hunger or starvation on them. In the gloaming light they started back to the monastery It was not far to go but Colum Cille had to sit down by the path to rest.

'God rested on the seventh day, Diarmad. And now the six days of my own work are past. Tomorrow, in the Sabbath of death I will rest. This my last night.' At these words a stream of tears fell down Diarmad's face. His body heaved with sobs. 'Let these sad tears baptize my going also with joy, that I shall be born into the sweet glens of paradise.'

At that moment the white horse that carried milk for the monks came to Colum Cille and rested and nuzzled its head on his breast, shedding great tears onto his cheeks. Long in this sorrow of lamentation as for the loss of a loved one the white horse stood, head bowed on the breast of Colum Cille, until Diarmad tried to shift the creature.

'Diarmad, this animal that has no speech divines my going and bids farewell. You with the gift of words and understanding I had to tell. Let the creature be.' After these words the white horse turned slowly, and walked into the meadow by the shore.

Colum Cille climbed a little hillock by the monastery. One last look he took at the silk soft sea and breathed the wild flower fragrance of the air and gazing skywards made this prophecy:

This place small and mean
though it be, will be
held in the highest honour not
by the Scots only but by the
rulers and peoples of foreign
nations and those lands with
other gods. The holy men of
other religions will give this
island reverence.

Weak and tired, with Diarmad supporting him, he came slowly down the hill to his cell to finish the last words he was copying from his beloved psalter:

They that seek the Lord shall not want
for anything that is good.

He laid down his quill and said, 'Now Baithene must take up this quill and continue the work.' (Upon the death of Colum Cille Baithene would become the abbot of Iona.) In the old man's mind he saw a little red squirrel with its bushy tail splashing water on the shore. Smiling he lay down on his pillow of stone, and with only Diarmad for companion he spoke (for the last time) keeping silence after, till his death:

I command to you, my little children
these my last words,
love one another unfeignedly. Peace.

The bell rang for the midnight office. Colum Cille rose and hastened before the others to the altar. He knelt in prayer. As Diarmad followed it seemed the holy man shone with light. He turned to face his brothers in Christ. A look of peace and joy was on his face. Diarmad held up his master's right hand to bless the choir of monks and, as much as he could, the saintly Colum Cille moved his hand to bless the brethren. Then, with no word spoken, his hand and body lost their strength and in quietness and peace his spirit left this world.

Three nights and three days the monks kept vigil over the saint's body and his face was peaceful as a sleeping child's. With sonorous chanting they wrapped the body in fine linen and buried Colum Cille within the walls of the monastery.

Yet one last strange journey took the body of the holy man to his native Erin. The Viking Mandor, son of the king of Lochlan, with war fleet attacked Iona, slew monks, plundered the abbey, tore up graves and tombs in search of treasure. With them to sea they took the coffin of Colum Cille, thinking to find treasure. On the foam-flecked sea these predators tore open the coffin and, finding the body, closed it and cast it into the waves. Onto the shore of Downpatrick in Erin it drifted and there the Abbot of Down discovered it. Colum Cille was then, as St Patrick and St Brigid prophesied, buried there with his brother and sister saints in hallowed ground. Others there are who say the body of the saint rests still in the holy island of Iona.

III

Celtic Folk and
Fairy Tales

A Door in the Wind

HE ALWAYS SAID it was the little starving man: that was where it all began, with the little shilpit Glasgow man who had no work, who had dossed in a household of other hungry men, who like himself could find no work. George of the golden tongue, the carrying voice of Colum Cille, he who in the open air could hold the ear of hundreds, on that day at four o'clock in the afternoon in a street in Govan, was preaching to five hundred men, men with nothing to do, no work to go to. Amongst them was a bone-thin man, threadbare of dress but clear of eye.

'Do you think this religious stuff will save? Do you trust the words you speak?'

The echo of his own doubts rasped in George's mind, 'Do I believe the words I say, do I do what I say? Does the Church?' These questions rang and rasped and, looking into the clear eyes of that dishevelled man, he thought, 'He is the preacher, not I.'

Some short time later George was called to a hospital to the bedside of a man dying, dying of starvation, a man who weekly sent a third of the pittance of his dole money to his feckless brother in Australia, a man who had left the household of his fellow unemployed because he thought he was eating too much of the shared rations. This man's name was Archie Gray, his heckler from the street in Govan.

'I wouldnae cross the doorway o' yer church. It's no because you don't preach the truth. It's because ye don't mean whit ye say.'

The meeting with this Archie Gray, this bone thin sacrifice, was the founding impulse. Here was the seed. Was it for this that young men in millions had died in the carnage of what was to be known as the First World War, for this 'the flooer o' the forest were a weed awa?' A place could surely be found, not for the destruction and hatred of war, but for the creativity of love and peace, a place where a community could live, mean what they said, and do what they believed.

Two seeds grew side by side in the mind of George MacLeod. Two great doubts planted two small seeds . . .

As he looked at the men in shabby clothes, saw their shoulders droop, their children pinched and crippled by rickets, the badges of hunger, he recalled the days such men, held upright by the call of their country to war, had been heroes, fibred by untold braveries. He, their captain, had led them to be maimed or killed in the mud and blood in the battle of Ypres, thirty thousand in one week, ten times the number of those whose blood was on the head and in the heart of Colum Cille fourteen hundred years before. 'What if,' whispered the voice of this first great doubt, 'that war you championed, that pinned medals on your chest, pride in your heart, had been one enormous mistake? And was this the better world these young men fought and died for, this hungry broken place, without purpose or hope?' The doubt would not leave his mind. *Dulce et decorum est pro patria mori* ran tinkling hollow now as did the vapid politician's promise of 'a land fit for heroes'. Here he was, preaching hope in these Glasgow streets where the poet Edwin Muir had 'walked from work each day through a slum filled with a sense of degradation and at last with an immense blind dejection.'

'And what of that church of your ancestors?' insistently whispered the second doubt, 'this church that you espouse, are wedded to, does it do as this dead scrap of bones has done, this Archie Gray, give life itself for love of friends?'

It was not in a quiet man these doubts found ground but in one not unlike that Columba of old, a man 'impatient, impulsive, poetic, awesome', driven by fierce passion and fearless when aroused. Yet now blind dejection and breakdown took hold of him. In solitude he wept.

It was spring time, April bursting with its sweet flowers, and George was on a boat with his father bound for the Holy Land, a voyage of healing; what waited, unimaginable. Sailing away from Scotland he was to enter a glittering Ali Baba's cave.

It was Easter morning, warm in the cloisters of the Russian Orthodox Church. George was in no mood for a lengthy ritual and intended to leave early.

Out of the silence in the church rose voices, harmonious, a hidden choir. The gates of the inner sanctuary flung open, two bearded young priests, hair flowing, bounded to meet the patriarch; from within burst out glorious song, a joy filled greeting. Nimble sprightly springtime . . . all rushed, flashes of colour, into the sanctuary. In the cascade suddenly, bearing one candle amongst many, in a glitter of light George followed. 'Christ is risen!' Every sound and action; music, incense, ritual, sang it loud: 'Christ is risen!' Time stopped. Priests sang to the patriarch, the patriarch to the priests. Each person in that congregation was informed as if it was the news of that very moment. 'He is risen! Christ is risen!'

The drama was perfect. Every sense in George was burnished. It was his epiphany, his resurrection. Morning had passed into afternoon, afternoon into evening, evening to night and at quarter to four in the morning, fresh as dew on the morning grass George walked back to the King David Hotel in Jerusalem. He had intended to leave early, but not early in the morning!

Iona was ablaze with summer when George came home across the little ferry from Fionnphort and put his feet once more upon her. It was the time of the long gloaming light, the waters shining with the colours of the pulsing sky, scarlet, yellow, wild, a kaleidoscope of wonder, a dance, rushing clouds, their shadows leaping up the mountainside. The glory of the west was in it.

At a door in the wind on Iona, where the veil is thin, the sea waves laughing white onto the shore, here on the oldest rock of the world he stood. Before him rose the martyr ghosts of St Oran and of Archie Gray. There in that place of the burial of kings, a place echoing with the voice of his ancestors and his own childhood memories, God spoke to George MacLeod. Here like a prince crowned by the elements of earth and air and water and fiery sun, each sense in the man sang alive.

As he gazed at the tussling waves it was as if he could see the sea-troubled coracle of Colum Cille beach on the shingle, scrape on the scratching pebbles, jewel glittering in the sun. Through a door in the wind he heard the voice of the eternal and in that thin place the wonder of creation filled him with prayer:

> Almighty Creator,
> The morning is yours, rising into fullness
> The summer is yours, dipping into autumn
> Eternity is yours, dipping into time.
> The vibrant grasses, the scent of flowers,
> The lichen on the rocks, the tang of seaweed,
> All are yours.
> Gladly we live in the garden of your creation.

Clad in the mantle of priest and seanachaidh a clearness seemed to sharpen his senses to the glory that was the Creator. A great company are around us, unknown men lost in coracles on westerns seas; St Columba and his community of monks sallied forth from here and returned for their refreshing. As he stood on that shore the poem made by Saint Columba, close to his time of death came into his mind:

> Iona of my heart, Iona of my love
> Instead of monks' voices there shall be
> The lowing of cattle; but ere the world
> Comes to an end, Iona shall be as it was.

A swell of love for this island rose like a tide in the heart of George MacLeod, a desire to help, like the little red squirrel of legend, to waken this prophetic dream into reality. Like the words to the Gaelic melody from Bunessan on the adjacent island of Mull 'Morning has broken like the first morning', the yellow-beaked blackbird sang anew the song of creation, a new dawn and new tomorrows were calling. It was a recreated man who, like Colossus, bestrode the little world of Iona the sunlong day. Nothing was impossible and to be alive was very heaven. Here was a cathedral roofed by the infinite skies, a choir of seabirds swooping and rushing like the young priests in Jerusalem, under the glowing patriarch of the sun. Waves chanted on the rocks. At night the candle stars and lady moon would come. Time was told in the ritual of the tides, the falling leaves, the setting sun, the rising moon. The glitter of the spirit was in birds, flowers and trees; all living things were the Creator's. Singing voices. Here was the pageant of the east on these western shores, the Celtic world and that celebration day of Easter in Jerusalem were one vision to be rekindled by the driving force of George MacLeod!

Into his mind came the words of his hero, Colum Cille's great dying prophecy: 'Unto this place, small and mean though it be, great homage shall yet be paid, not only by the kings and people of the Scots, but by the rulers of foreign and barbarous nations and their subjects. In great veneration too shall it be held by holy men of other churches.'

Echo and re-echo of these words, as if carried in the waves of the sea, broke on the shore of his consciousness. He would play his part in fulfilling the prophecy held like a crucible of adventure and hope in these words. Adventure!

The sun rose, the dew dried as he walked the island, gazed from Dun I across the sea, saw Bride of the Isles glimpse the lovely face of the Virgin in the well of youth: like Macbeth, beheld the pageant of the burial of many kings as the sun made its golden pathway on the sea. In the long slow falling of dusk he came by the ghost-gliding cloisters of the ruined nunnery where flitted shadows of the attentive holy women tending gardens of herbs, keeping full the chalice of prayer, blessing with their care and prayer the circle of all living things, mothers of mercy to the troubled world.

As dark drew on at last he came to the beckoning ruins of the Abbey, seeming to rebuild itself in the silver of the rising moon. It was as if the very stones of the Abbey spoke to him, 'Why does someone not rebuild me?' Faint at first the voice, 'Like a simmering kettle when it first begins to whistle,' he thought, until 'the very lid of that kettle was rattling . . . ' Didn't the stones shout through the gap of silence, these most uncomfortable of ruins, 'Who will build me again, give life to the prophecy spoken by that warrior of God exiled from Ireland's shore? And you an exile from conformity, is this sea-girt isle not a place to bring your dreams to harbour, give truth to the little starving man you met to accuse you, you so fine with words, the darling of the safe and comfortable pews, so break, break loose again, the coracle will find its way ashore.'

He knew what he must do.

As if to give the conviction no time to sleep, he saw within the Abbey, a little light, and creeping close, like Tam O'Shanter to Kirk Alloway, he saw a wondrous sight. A single candle set upon a little harmonium, and round that dim glow five adults and three children singing, singing the twenty third psalm. He was deeply moved by the reverence of this tiny family congregation singing in the ruins. As dreamed of by Columba he determined this place should be a Church for no less than all the family of God. 'Get on with it,' spoke the voices in George's head. 'Be bold and resolute!'

His brave new world was to quell the dragon doubts that now breathed fire on his convictions, his aspiration no less than to have a Christ community that did as it said, put its money where its mouth was, and out of the destruction in the aftermath of war brought creativity and a Community of Peace. Unemployed craft and trades-men of Govan and Clydeside would be wedded at the altar of rebuilding the Abbey to fledgling ministers of the Church. It was to be an interesting marriage. The great matchmaker and idealist was a disciple too of the poetry of practicality. He needed money and was not blate in seeking it in the pockets of the rich. 'Give me tainted money, and I will untaint it,' asserted his conviction. 'Whenever I pray, coincidences multiply.' Foxy cunning, a poet's tongue, a field commander's boldness and strategies were not poor credentials, neither for his mission, nor to help coincidences multiply.

Sir James Lithgow was one of Scotland's richest men and so full, in the reverend Captain George's sights, not withstanding the awkwardness that he had, on grounds of his pacifism, refused to offer a blessing on the launch of a battleship built by Sir James. Planning his campaign of rebuilding the Abbey, George Macleod proposed to encamp his reconstruction troops in wooden huts around the Abbey. To provide them, money was required.

In a leisurely yacht trip round the Western Isles with his wife

Sir James, had, in passing Iona, remarked to Lady Lithgow: 'I wonder that no one rebuilds the rest of the Abbey.'

'And, how would they go about it?' said she.

Whereupon her husband placed chocolate sweeties representing wooden huts around a drawing of the ruins, 'Here would be the workers' huts!'

When the bold dragon slayer entered their house with an identical scheme and sketch in hand, Sir James was already pleased to advance money for his own idea, a sweet coincidence!

The stone quarry in Mull was owned by the Duke of Argyll who opposed this upstart churchman's scheme. Land in Iona outside the confines of the Abbey precincts Argyll also owned. No stone was to be taken from his quarry and no water to be piped from his land! 'Since you have neither water nor stone, your project cannot proceed.'

Without water there was no life. Without stone nothing could be built. It was a dark day, darker still when water diviners failed to locate a source within the Abbey grounds. The steamer to take them from the island was delayed, and to pass the time they fell to digging outside the west door of the Abbey church in hope of finding coins. They found the treasure of a well! When it was opened fully, from it gushed a Jordan of water, four hundred gallons a day, a glorious baptism.

And then, and then the stones in the boundary wall round the Abbey spoke. A little man from Govan who could have been an Archie Gray, saw that these time-weathered stones were from the ruined Abbey, better far than any stone new-hewn from Mull. Perfect. And so the work went on.

Then in 1939 came war with Germany. It demanded and requisitioned every available spar of timber and certainly none could be made available for rebuilding an Abbey on a remote Scottish island, in a scheme championed by a religious pacifist.

A great sea storm in the Atlantic, a year later, forced a Swedish ship to jettison its cargo of Canadian timber which floated conveniently to Mull just opposite Iona and the timber cut precisely to the required length. Life was not dull. Coincidences multiplied. Twice more for the roof of refectory and cloisters, the 'usual miracles' brought timber to the builders of the Abbey on one occasion en route from Ireland, that green Ireland from whence Columba came to Iona! At last the fabric of dream was translated to stone, mortar, walls, roof, an Abbey, the glory of the West, and inhabiting it, a community espousing the ideals of the ancient Celtic church.

By now our man George is Lord George MacLeod, ex moderator of the Church of Scotland and so The Very Reverend, Lord George MacLeod. He is, with his wife Lorna and their three children, on a peaceful ecumenical church cruise to the Mediterranean and the Holy Land. It is an easeful family pilgrimage and already they have had an audience in Rome with the Pope, with Archbishop Makarios in Cyprus, visited Jerusalem, Tiberias and Ephesus. Sailing on the blue Mediterranean they arrive in Athens.

A little frisson of unease might be felt in the early morning breeze on this May morning. Greece was in control of the repressive regime of the colonels and word is about of their secret prisons, detention without trial and rumours of ill-treatment and torture. They have removed the Metropolitan of the Cathedral of Athens and installed their own man in that office. For this reason George has made it quietly but vividly clear to the group organizer, Canon Payton, that their party should attend no official reception in Athens with the Metropolitan of the Cathedral. Canon Payton gives him this assurance and the ecumenical party divides and sets off on seven separate sightseeing tours. The day is warm and pleasant and relaxed and the Canon sits at ease with a fine Greek coffee. Not for long. His reverie is interrupted by the arrival of an excited Archbishop James, Dean of the Greek Cathedral in London, bearing the awkward news that the Metropolitan and his bishops await their presence in the Cathedral at noon.

Canon Payton decides that the wisest course is to accept the invitation, and the most diplomatic, not to inform the Very Reverend Lord George MacLeod. All the groups apart from that of the leader of the Iona community are informed and dutifully arrive in the Cathedral for the twelve noon appointment.

Speeches of welcome commence within the cool vaults of the Cathedral. Suddenly to the eyes of Canon Payton the whole world moves into a nightmarish slow motion. He is here, resplendent in rainbow shirt. He is marching down the centre aisle, his eyes ablaze. A cool anger, controlled and dangerous. He is ready to pull the pin and launch the grenade. He does.

Despite a vociferous but ineffectual rearguard of protest from the Canon and Archbishop Dean, Lord George's slow fuse of eloquence fills the Cathedral reaching a climactic explosion as he denounces the demonic practices of the regime of the Colonels. 'Is the Archbishop blind and deaf to the cruelty and torture being meted out to innocent people?'

An unholy silence settles. The Metropolitan is skulking out of sight behind the screen of the sanctuary. Relentless, Captain George harries him. 'Will you or your bishops not give an answer? Is silence your answer of complicity?' Like chidden children the congregation scatter into the afternoon sunshine.

Let not the left hand know . . . The everyday life of the Iona Community had a Columban order and discipline, busy. One of its members, Ann Smith, had an eye condition which she had been told could mean that if her sight failed for more than an hour it probably never would return. Another community member found her, head in hands, softly weeping, hours had passed and her sight had not returned. This man fetched George MacLeod. Unflurried, unhurried, he asked the member to place his hands on her head. Over these he placed his own and with his powerful voice and poet's tongue he prayed for healing.

Almost at once, tears streaming down her face, she shouted in a pure ecstatic Glasgwegian accent, 'O my God, I can see!'

'Don't be talking about this!' said the healer. This was not the first nor the last of his healing, but he was insistent that the news should not be noised abroad, a little bit of contrast to the uproar that was the general habit of his life!

George MacLeod's son Maxwell was six or seven years old. He was peacefully asleep of a fine morning in Iona. A long lie was not his father's plan.

'Time to rise, the morning is singing; listen to the breeze in the trees, the seals are waiting, the curlew is calling, far out at sea the great gannet is gliding, they all are singing the song of Iona. Come! I have people I have argued with.' When was he not in some battle of words or principles? 'We are to meet at the shore. The swim in this wave of the Atlantic will be our baptism of forgiving.'

Up rose the bewildered six year old to join in this mad morning frolic in the chill Atlantic waves. And there at the shore the reluctant co-celebrants were gathered in this ritual of forgiveness, or was it to appease the tyrant? And then at the Atlantic's rim, bursting into the breakers of the whale's-shrine sea, plunged the porpoise George MacLeod followed by his shivery son and reluctant builder-priests and community members.

Above them wheel and screech the herring gulls, far out the gannet glides hunting on the wind currents. The breeze rustles the grasses of the machair; it is Columba's world of one and a half millennia ago. Baptised by the chill Atlantic, out from the water wades the grinning porpoise, while his girning companions and chattering child spurt for the comforts of towel, and clothes, and warmth, and shelter, and breakfast.

'You are forgiven!' he roars at their vanishing heels.

For himself, roof of sky and walls of wind are the Great Creator's Abbey; the seashore rustle of pebble and wave and birdsong, music enough. On the altar of the sea's edge he kneels and prays, gives thanks for this most complete of worlds. It is a thin place, a tissue membrane only separating earth from heaven. To his little son he wishes to bequeath Columba's kingdom, the consciousness of the Celts, the celebration of all things, for even the stones are alive.

Years later, a pipe tune and the memory of these days playing in his mind, days when his father had told him stories at the summit of Dun I, taken him into the breath-taking Atlantic, wakened him from the fantasy of dreams to the poetry of the living world,

Maxwell Macleod made the words of this song and put it to a tune of the Scottish bagpipes, 'O mo Ghaoil' (O my Love):

> The isle of our dreams becomes real with the morning
> The grey dawn moves on, new tomorrows are calling
> We smile as we wake and sigh as the wind –
> Sing the quiet song of Iona.
>
> And soft on the breeze we hear the gulls screaming
> The sound of the trees swaying and moving
> And the waves on the beach, as they ebb and they flow
> Sing the quiet song of Iona.
>
> And far out at sea the great gannet is gliding
> His wings need not move for the rhythm he's feeling
> And the seal is a song as he turns in the wave –
> He is the quiet song of Iona.
>
> So let us be quiet, part of the fullness,
> Let us belong to the glorious completeness,
> So that we may return to the island and then
> Sing the quiet song of Iona.

'Rage, rage against the dying of the light.' (Dylan Thomas) The Very Reverend Lord George Macleod was prowling and growling about the house in Learmonth like a creature caged by the infirmities of age; impatient, impotent and irritated, much to be done and less capacity and time to do it. So his son Max, thinking to occupy and pacify the old warrior, took him on a trip to France, to Taize, where were gathered peaceable and peace-seeking folk of the spirit. Here were arranged lectures on topics of a spiritual nature. Lord George was to give a lecture on the third day.

At one of these talks Max left his father and betook himself gratefully to a field of meditation, relieved to be briefly rid of the beloved unexploded bomb that was his father. Not for long. Deaf, and finding the role of audience did not suit him, Lord George arose and commenced thundering a lecture on pacifism to the dumbstruck lecturer and assembly. A messenger rushed and relayed to Max this news. Max raised his hands in a shrug of 'don't ask me' and would dearly have loved to disclaim at that moment any knowledge of the dreadful man.

The next day the identical scenarios were re-enacted, so that the defeated organisers in despair surrendered the podium at once to Lord George, who burst into fire in flames of persuasive eloquence on the cause of pacifism. All seats were taken; young and old stood rapt, prisoners of the old man's blaze, and rattle, and poetry, and all at last applauded loud and long as the gruff general left one of his last battlefields.

He was growing old, his prowess failing, but his will and spirit were still of steel. In this time of the dying of the light at last he was confined to bed, and to comfort his last hours his son invited a musician to play harp music, thinking perhaps, as David had of old soothed the heart of a king, this music would quieten the spirit of this majestic man of God. For hours in the quietness the musician played. A blessed silence fell and the old man's eyes were closed in rest.

When the harper left, Max asked, 'Father, did you like the music of the harp?'

'What did you say?' said the dying lion.

'Did you like it, the harp music?' shouted Max.

'It was awful!' bellowed Lord George, 'awful!'

Later in the small hours of the night he died. Doubtless into heaven the soul of the great, wild, good warrior exploded, through the gates amongst the startled congregation, to continue marshalling and leading arguments in some celestial cause.

Colum Cille of Ireland and Iona, Lord George MacLeod of Fuinary and Iona: born fourteen hundred years apart and yet with such consanguinity of spirit and traits of character, the two might have been brothers. Each was an aristocratic warrior Celt in spirit; each led men to death in battle, and thereafter devoted life and soul to finding conscripts for the Christ God. Each was a mighty man, with love of poetry, flyting, argument, wit and words. Each was endowed with a giant's voice and poet's tongue. Each was a charismatic leader, impulsive, fierce, compassionate. Each without compromise made entrenched enemies and devoted followers. Each left the loch of life still.

Over Nine Waves

FOR LONG AND LONG, no man nor woman know the length of that time, the Tuatha Dé Danann, the people of the goddess Danu, held rule and sway over Ireland. These people were half gods and bore powers of spells, enchantments and magic. But at the last they were put from that place.

In ships from afar came the sons of the shining arrow, the very gentle ones, afterwards called the Sons of the Gael. Their leader was Miled after whom these people got also the name of the Milesians. It was said that by treachery the Tuatha Dé Danann had slain Ith, a high prince among the Sons of the Gael. It was to avenge his death that they came to invade Ireland. The people of Miled came in good heart, for by the druids had it been prophesied that when they came to this green island in the west they would possess it, and even if they failed it would be a land possessed by their children. And so from the south, under the leadership of Miled, to the shores of Invershane came the men and women warriors of the Gaels. To defend that shore flocked the people of the Tuatha Dé Danann.

By their enchantments the Dé Danann druids cast over the whole island a whirling mist and over the Sons of the Gael a dizziness of confusion. They raised above them a great cloud in shape of a wild boar, eyes like red suns glaring from it, as if ready to charge thundering from the skies. So northwards along the coast fled the ships of the Sons of the Gael. In Munster, the hero Amergin, son of Miled, came ashore and there met severally with three Irish queens, wide-eyed and of matchless beauty. With three kings too he spoke and was in great wonder, for these three brothers shared the rule of that green and sweet meadowed land, and were in warlike dispute brother against brother. It was strange to Amergin that they should be in quarrels in such a land, so fruitful the forests, so full of fish the rivers, the sun neither too strong nor the cold too bitter. Boldly Amergin spoke at a gathering of the brothers in a court of great grandeur.

'In recompense for the treachery with which you slew our kins-man, the high Prince Ith, we demand that you surrender to us the kingship of this land . . . or in battle the matter will be settled.'

The boldness of these words amazed these brothers of the Tuatha Dé Danann. 'Our army is not yet ready,' said they, 'but we see you are a man of good judgement and wisdom. Put to us an offer of terms. If that offer is not just, with enchantments we will destroy you and your people.'

Then Amergin made this offer: 'My men, my fleet and all my people will sail from your island the length of nine waves from the shore. If you then can hinder us from landing on your island we will return to our own land, but if you fail you will surrender your kingship and be under the sway of my people.'

This offer pleased the people of the Tuatha Dé Danaan for they were sure that their power over wind and sea, and dark enchant-ments would destroy and scatter the enemy. True to their word the Sons of the Gael drew up anchors and moved out to the length of nine waves from the shore. At once the druids of the people of the Tuatha Dé Danann took to their deepest spells and enchantments and cast winds of fury over sea and land; the tempestuous storms battered the boats of the Sons of the Gael. Ships were tossed like cork on the waves, dashed and broken to pieces on rocks, men were washed into the sea by giant waves and drowned. Five of the eight sons of Miled met their death in that enchanted tempest. And Amergin, son of Miled, seeing this fury of storm to be the work of spells, put his own blessing on the waters and upon his people. Standing boldly in the prow of his ship he said: 'May those who now toss on the great wide food-giving sea reach safely to land. May they find a place upon its plains and valleys, in its forests, full of nuts and fruits, its rivers and lakes full of fish. May our chief men and learned women confront the great Queen Erin, noble of blood.'

When he had spoken the wind died down and the sea in a moment was quiet. And Amergin, first of them all, came on the shore of Ireland and said,

I am the wind that breathes upon the sea
I am the wave of the ocean
I am the murmur of the billows
I am the ox of the seven combats
I am the vulture upon the rocks
I am a beam of the sun
I am the fairest of plants
I am a wild boar in valour
I am a salmon in the water
I am a lake in the plain
I am the word of knowledge
I am the point of the spear in battle
I am the God who created in the head the fire.
Who is it who throws light into the gathering on the mountain?
Who announces the age of the moon?
Who teaches the place where the sun rests?
(If not I)

In three days three great battles were fought between the peoples of the Tuatha De Danann and the Sons of the Gael. Many were the dead on each side. On the afternoon of the third day Amergin rose on a hillock and reminded his people of the treachery that brought the death of their kinsman Ith. At this the battle fury came into the Sons of the Gael and utterly they routed the Tuatha De Danann leaving but few alive. Those survivors of the people of Danu would in no way suffer to be under the sword of Miled and the Sons of the Gael. They sought therefore the great knowledge and enchantments of Manannan son of Lir, the great sea god, to find them secret places, safe from their enemies.

Manannan chose out for them the most beautiful hills and valleys of all Ireland for their secret homes. Around these he put hidden walls through which no mortal man could see. Only the people of Danu could see and pass through these walls.

For these people also he made the feast of Age, food and drink that bore enchantments. The ale he brewed kept those who drank of it from age, from sickness, and from death. The food of that feast was of Manannan's own swine that, though killed and eaten on one day, the next would once more be alive.

So it is told that long and long ago, no man nor woman knowing the length of that time, the people of the goddess Danu fled before the Sons of the Gael to the hillocks, mounds, and glens of Erin and of Alba. There girt by the invisible walls of Manannan they dwell and are the sídhe, or fairy folk. It is how we mortals serve them and their dwelling places for kindness or ill that they will bring blessings or evil fortune upon our lives, for they are folk with the power of hidden worlds. Since these far times they have appeared in many forms, to meddle with or mind the destiny of earthly folk.

At the time of the year when day and night and light and dark are equal, the walls of the sídhe are thinnest, and at these times it is given to certain mortals to see and to have dealings with the people of the sídhe.

Hunter of the Yellow Grouse

LONG LONG SINCE as legend tells, the people of the goddess Danu fled before the sons of the Gaels to the safety of the loveliest glens, and hillocks, and mounds, of Erin and Alba. There the sea god Manannan mac Lir surrounded their secret places with invisible walls only they could go through. There they dwell, the daoine sídhe, the 'fairy folk'. Ever since these misty times it is how we mortals welcome or spurn them that they bring good or bad fortune to our days. In some of these sídhe folk is a heart yearning for a mortal creature and it is well known that a woman of their kind will fasten her desire upon a mortal man.

Upon a hill in the highlands of Scotland lived a banshee, 'fairy woman'. This hill too, was the favourite hunting ground of one of the greatest hunters ever on the bens and glens of the Gaidhealtachd, so great his fame that far to the Outer Hebrides even he was known as Sealgair a'Choilich Bhuidhe, 'the hunter of the yellow grouse'. Silent as moonlight on grass, swift as the deer on the high hill, eye of the golden eagle, none was his match. Strong his stretch on bowstring, far the flight of his arrow; no wild fowl in the heavens above that would not be pierced and brought to earth by the tip of his arrow. A bird but a speck in the sky would fall to the darting arrow of Sealgair a'Choilich Bhuidhe. With bow, arrow, hunting knives, spears, and axes in the gloaming light of the mouth of the morning he was a faint and silent shadow on the face of the hill. His quarry the yellow grouse, black cock, moor hen, ptarmigan, roebuck and, greatest of prizes, the wild boar of the glens. In the dew-fresh morning always he was upon the hill, and never did he return with an empty hand, such a man was the hunter of the yellow grouse.

Then as the sunset was below the hill one evening he returned with nothing, not beast nor fowl, a strange sight to his four brothers and his mother's eyes. And on the days that followed the same: in the morning with bow and arrow, hunting knives, spear, and axes he would go and, as night darkened, return with neither yellow grouse, his dearest, nor moor hen, wild boar nor even a rabbit nor a hare. With nothing he returned and nothing he spoke of his hunting on the hill. Yet each day he set off, seeming ever eager as before and each night with nothing he returned. It seemed that he grew pale and a farness was in his eye.

It was this his mother saw and feared. She feared with her inner sight that he was taken, taken by the woman of the sídhe; that he was in the thrall of her love, and this she saw as she gazed into the peat fire flames. She saw the meeting of the eldest son, Sealgair a'Choilich Bhuidhe, the first and foremost of her heart, and his eyes only for the fairy woman. This in the flames she saw. She wrung her hands and with tears her eyes burned.

'Better he were dead,' she whispered to herself, 'than be taken by a banshee to the people of the other side, the fairy folk beyond the veil of mortal seeing.'

It was the youngest brother who heard the whisper of his mother's words. Before the sun had taken the dew from the grass in the morning, following his custom, Sealgair a' Choilich Bhuidhe left for the hill. With all the skills of old, darting between rocks, crouching, crawling, sheltering from sight the four brothers came after him as he made his fixed way up the glen and onto the hill. Behind a great rock the brothers hid and there in a hollow on the hilltop they saw what human eyes were never meant to see. They saw her, fine, and strange, and lovely, in the morning glow; hair rippling in the little breeze. And there they saw the great hunter Sealgair a'Choilich Bhuidhe, the hunter of the yellow grouse, embrace and kiss her. As if to fetch some token, the woman of the sídhe left this brother and into the hillside she went. At this moment, impelled by his mother's words and grief, the youngest drew and let loose an arrow. Swift as falcon falls upon its prey it took its mark and pierced the neck of Sealgair a'Choilich Bhuidhe. In the hollow of the hillside the hunter of the yellow grouse spilled his life's blood and lay there dead. The brothers went down from the hill.

At that time of the morning of the raven's croak, as if divining this dark deed, out from the hillside came again the woman of the sídhe. When her eye fell on her lover, blood from his neck, blood from his mouth, spilling upon the heather hill, and he without the breath of life there came from her a wild keening, shrill and knife-sharp. The arrow of pain was in her heart and from her grief she sang:

It is I am full of grief for
Sealgair a'Choilich Bhuidhe
my hunter of the yellow grouse;
did I not hear you cry upon the brae,
yet to it I paid no heed when they came for you
not till I heard the croak of the raven's voice.
A thousand curses fall upon the brothers,
a thousand curses on those who put this sight to my eyes
blood from your body, blood from your neck
and you now lying stretched still in the hollow.

She finished her song and her wailing put tears on the wind.

Leannán Sídhe

NOT SO VERY long ago in Antrim there lived a young man named Randall Mcquillan, and oh, was he not the handsome one; big he was and strong and broad of the shoulder, narrow hips and hair black as a raven's wing. Nut brown was his skin. Long and black his eye lashes and his eyes a twinkle of blue. If that was not enough, the song in his mouth was a river of pure gold. Not a lass or young woman in the country was not mad for him and sure that was no wonder, for men like him are as scarce as golden eagles. But it was not the eyes of mortals only that were taken with the beauty of Randall McQuillan.

One moonlit night as he was walking from Ballycastle over the hill and across the moor, he was followed close and close by a leannán sídhe, a fairy woman. She sighed, and she cried, and she plucked at his coat to make him look at her, but he would not turn round for he knew that if he once looked on her face, his soul would be forever lost, and he forever in her thrall. So he stood still, pulled his cap over his eyes, and steadfastly refused to look. There he waited, still as a stone. At last she left him and drifted on her way over the moorland.

Only when he was sure that she had gone did he lift his head, push his cap back from his eyes and walk on. But look, look! There she was, clear in the silver of the moon, a bright shadow on a distant hill, gazing round, bending, hiding something under an ancient standing stone. As Randall watched, a veil of mist swirled around her. When it lifted she was gone.

Slowly, as if in a dream, he made his way home. That night he dreamed again and again of a swirling of mist; it plucked at his coat, tugged at him, and pulled him towards a bright shadow, bending and beckoning him to come to the old standing stone on the moon-pale hillside. Cold and moist in the morning he woke, the beckoning figure haunting him. He put salt in one pocket and iron in another to ward off the enchantment, and over the moor to the place of the standing stone he made his way.

OUT OF THE MOUTH OF THE MORNING

Growing close by the great stone was a bush, yellow with broom, and there, peeping a little out and hidden under the bush, he found a casket made of leather and full to the brim with golden coins. He carried it home and buried it under an elder tree, for he knew that the fairy folk could not touch it there.

Still every night she came crying, and sighing, and wailing, and sobbing, after him; though he never once lifted his eyes to look at her. Never would he look in her face, but never would she give him rest or peace. Always when he was alone, when he was walking home over the moor, she was there plucking at his coat, pleading, wailing.

Now, living in Ballycastle was a young woman named Nancy McDonald whose beauty and lilting ways had taken Randall's heart. For long he had wanted to ask her to make a life with him. Perhaps if he were married he would be free of the beseechings of the unearthly leannán sídhe! So one night Randall asked Nancy to marry him and she agreed. The very next evening he would talk to her father, who kept the village inn and thought more of himself than anything else in the world.

'You'll marry none of him,' said he to her, 'for what has he to offer you but a few hungry acres and a scattering of mountain sheep, a thatch that wants mending is poor shelter in the winter's day. You'll have none of him while I have a breath in me!'

Well, Randall was proud enough himself and much hurt by this refusal. So soon he let it be known about the countryside, and dropped a few words in the inn, that he had a store of gold coins.

'Troth, the only gold you'll ever see is on the buttercups in the field,' said her father, but when Randall brought the leather casket to the inn one night he piped a different tune.

'Now my lad, that will be treasure trove for sure and if the authorities was to find out about that, well, deep, deep, trouble you would be in. Now we wouldn't want that to happen to a fine young man like yourself would we? And they would take it off you for sure. Now indeed we wouldn't want that to happen! I tell you what, to save you getting into any kind of trouble like that I could keep it safe for you and I will give you enough money to thatch the cottage and to put over for the wedding until we decide what best to do with the money.'

Randall gave him the gold willingly enough, for truth to tell he was glad to be rid of it for fear of the fairy host. So, in time, the two were married, and a fine and handsome couple they made. A fine wedding it was, eating and drinking of the very best and the dancing, and singing, and music making, went on till the birds were singing in the bushes and the sunlight skipping in the grass.

But that night, when the honeymooners went to bed, the leannán sídhe made a sighing, and crying, and wailing, round the house. It was an eerie awful sound like the very wind weeping.

'Great heavens,' cried Nancy, 'what terrible thing is that?'

'It is nothing but the wind,' said Randall, 'it is only the wind, my love.'

And he closed her eyes with kisses, and she fell asleep in his arms . . . but an eerie glow shone at the window. And through the night came a crying so filled with pain and longing that it broke the heart. If it was the wind itself, sure, it was like the keening of a woman who has known the grief of many deaths. Night after night around the house sounded the wild wailing of the leannán sídhe.

Now it was 'strange indeed' said the village people that 'they were married only seven days when Nancy's mother fell suddenly ill'.

'You must come and nurse her,' said her father, and so Nancy went down to Ballycastle to look after her sick mother, though the very day before was she not skipping like a spring lamb!

That night young Randall came back from the hill to an empty house, ate his dinner, and fell asleep by the fire. The moon rose and silver light streamed in through the window. He was wakened from his sleep by a long lonesome cry, a cry so filled with pain and longing that it would crack the heart of any man. He looked up and staring in through the window at him was the beautiful face of the leannán sídhe, pale as a water lily and lovelier than the moonlight itself. Drawn and held by that face Randall rose, rose from his chair, and followed her through the silver of the moonlight to the land of the sídhe.

An open door, the dishes from his supper, and ashes in the hearth, were all that was left to tell of him. Only the old women whispered that he was taken by the leannán sídhe.

'Did you not hear her keening?'

'I heard her for sure, wailing the long night.'

'And it the night of the big moon. Sure she has taken him, God rest the poor man.'

Though it seemed to him no more than the passing of a day it was seven long years before Randall came home and stood in the half light of evening outside his cottage door. He looked in the window and saw Nancy rocking a cradle and, sitting by the fire in his chair, a stranger. The door was locked, a thing unknown. He knocked, and Nancy came, and gazed at him as if himself was the stranger. He laughed.

'Who is our guest this night, Nancy, and whose the bairn?' She answered never a word. 'What welcome is this for your husband, lass?'

'My husband has been dead these seven years. Five long years I waited. Be gone, old man, you are none of mine!'

And then in the mirror over the mantelpiece Randall saw his reflection, his skin ashen and haggard, his hair, once black as the raven's wing, now white as snow. And there behind him glowing in the mirror ghostly and beautiful, pale as the water lily and lovelier than the moon . . . the face of the leannán síde. He uttered a soft howl of pain and turned and vanished into the darkness of the night. He never was seen again.

As for the gold in the casket of leather, they do say that when McDonald opened it there was nothing but a handful of dry beech leaves. They say too, that it would be better for a man to be drowned at sea than look in the face of the leannán sídhe, for he will wander the world after her for evermore. For the face of the fairy woman is lovelier than lilies, and her song sweeter than the lowing of calves on the warm hillside.

Fairy Wind

LONG AGO IN IRELAND there was a poor widow's son, and he served on a sailing ship voyaging from land to land around the world. No man alive was more handsome than he. 'Men like that are rare as the golden eagle,' the old women at home would say. He could do the work of any of your five men on board and forbye that no man was more courageous or cheerful than he, so no wonder that the Scottish skipper valued him high and treated him as his right hand man.

Far and wide, for years and years, they sailed the seas and at last were crossing the Atlantic home to Ireland. When the first seabird of Ireland was sighted floating and swooping over the sparkling sea, they knew it would not be long until they were cruising beneath the purple hills of Connemara. With the thought of home the Irishman filled the air with song.

Alas, that man was right who said, 'Three things there are cannot be trusted – the king, the sea, the weather.' In an hour the schooner was in the grips of a sudden and fierce storm. Through the dark of the day and the blackness of the night the storm howled and shrieked till the noon of the next day, and still it raged like a wild beast. The timbers were like to crack, and split, and let in the rushing sea. At any moment it seemed to the helpless crew the vessel could be drowned in the fury of the waves. Only the skill of the skipper, time and again, kept her afloat. But the creaking timbers spoke that the end was near.

Then, into the mind of the Scottish captain came the ancient story of Jonah, who put at hazard a whole ship's crew. 'Time was,' said he, 'when every man was lost on account of the bad luck on one.'

He ordered all hands on deck. And then cast lots and it fell out that the Irishman, like Jonah, was to be thrown into the sea. Aghast, the captain again cast lots, and yet again, and each time, the lot fell upon the Irishman. By now the vessel was fast in danger of sinking.

'Well now,' says the Irishman, 'better one man go than all be lost.'

Calm and cheerful in the storm's midst he made his way, smoking his last pipe, to the stern of the ship. In his hand he had his sailor's knife to cut tobacco. As he looked, a great mountain of wave rose above the ship. 'I'll not need this again,' said he and he hurled his knife into the very breast of the mighty wave.

As he did a gash of red appeared where the knife had pierced the wave, and the sea collapsed into a sudden peaceful calm. No more wind was in the air than would be in the spout of the kettle. The sails hung limp in the still and silent air. Becalmed upon that silent eerie sea the ship was motionless from noon that day, through all the dark and noiseless night, until noon of the next day, and on until the sun in orange and crimson gleams was falling down the sky.

The captain climbed to the crow's nest aloft, spy-glass in hand, and with it scoured the horizon of the sea. Suddenly he called down to the Irishman that a wonder was to be seen greater than any wonder that any man could see. He clambered down beside the Irishman and pointed along the orange and golden path made by the dying sun. There on the surface of the sea was a rider on a milk-white horse galloping in the direction where their vessel lay. Side by side they stood and saw horse and rider near the ship. They dropped the ladder and the gentleman, resplendent in gold braid came up and climbed aboard. He asked for words with the captain of the ship, and together they descended to the captain's cabin. There he told the captain that he'd come to ask him a favour for twenty-four hours.

'No trouble,' said the captain, 'no favour on board my vessel I would refuse you but for one and that is the Irishman; I will not part with that man.'

'It is the same man that I am seeking,' said the stranger, 'and I give you my hand and my word that I will bring him back safe and sound before the passing of one whole day is out. In that time your vessel will not stir an inch this way or that from where she is now until we return.'

'On that understanding,' said the captain, 'you can take him.'

Onto the head of the Irishman the gentleman placed a sea-cap and had him mount behind him on the horse, and then into the northwest on the orange-gold pathway of the setting sun they rode. Over the sea and down under the sea they rode. In all his living days never had the Irishman seen a land as strange or beautiful, trees and plants of luxurious foliage, giant flowers and then glittering buildings of strange and marvellous shape. Ever more magnificent were these buildings until they passed into a gorgeous palace that filled him with wonder. There he was welcomed with a hundred thousand welcomes and bade to await the feast that would be prepared.

As he sat in a daze of awe and amazement he heard from a nearby room such a mournful keening filled with pain and sadness that he rose and entered through a great door. There, lying raised on a fine bed, was a woman more beautiful than he had ever seen in all the wide world of his travels. In her breast was a knife.

'For the sake of pity and love itself,' said she, 'take out this knife from me.'

At once the young Irishman stepped forward and pulled out the knife from her breast. Then, gazing at the hilt, a black shame was on him, for on that hilt was carved – his name. 'Be feeling no shame,' said the young woman, now hale and well, 'for if you had not done as you did, I would have drowned the vessels and all who were in it.'

'Now, why such a desperate thing?' asked the Irishman.

'It is that as I flew as a bird of the air my eye fell upon you and my heart was taken with a quenchless love. I had to have you for my own!'

'Sure,' said the Irishman, 'any man would be proud to be your servant without you do such a desperate thing.'

'Ah!' said she, 'love is foolish, love is blind. We would do well to marry.'

'Mùs e, mùs e,' said he, 'now don't be mocking me a poor sailor.'

'It is no mockery!' said she. 'I know of you and your people and it is only your mother you have now, alone and poor and low in spirits in her little house.'

So they married and were happy and easy, and in great joy one with the other. Her name was Caitlín Tuirill. Then she fetched a casket of gold coins. 'Take this,' said she, 'and with it have a fine house built for your mother with land enough and near the sea.'

'Indeed, I will not be parted from you till I die,' said he.

'For one year and a night you will be parted from me, but now go you must, for my brother will not break his promise to the captain.'

Even as she spoke, her brother was knocking at the door, calling him. 'Leave us another quarter of an hour,' begged the lovely young woman.

They clung to each other kissing, and in sweet mourning at their parting, until it was time to go. He set off, springing upon the horse behind the gentleman, and together they rode; under the sea they rode and upon the sea until they sighted the vessel, and it still in the same location. The captain lowered the ladder over the side and the Irishman sprang for it.

'May your voyage prosper,' called the gentleman and off he sped across the sun gold path of sea.

Indeed immediately that he was gone the wind freshened enough to give them a speedy cruise to Galway Bay. It was late in the evening when he reached home. His mother was sitting in a recess, grieving, and no one was there but herself. He sat down and she did not recognize him, but was amazed that such a grand and noble looking person should come in.

'Mùs e, mother,' said he, 'is it how you don't recognize me, your own son?'

She jumped up and threw her arms around his neck and when she had wept her fill they sat talking until dawn. She ran out next day with all the excitement that was in her and gathered in the full of the house for a whole week. He bought her a farm of land, cattle and stock, and he built her a grand big house close in by the sea. However, he was but a month at home when he began to fail. None of the cures his mother was making could halt his decline.

He was withdrawn, living in a world of his own. He was forever composing a haunting song in honour of Caitlín Tuirill and neither his mother, nor any of the neighbours, knew who she was. It was exactly a year when his mother saw him grow easy, happy at last that his song was completed. He sang it for her with great tenderness and with shining face. As he finished, something caught her eye, flashing from the distant sandy shores.

She could have sworn she saw a girl on a white horse there but a sudden *sí gaoithe* 'fairy wind' flitting across the sunlit fields blocked her view. When it passed there was only the sparkling ocean. With a sigh she looked back. At first she thought him to be sleeping, so peaceful he looked, but he himself was away in the fairy wind.

The Tramp and the Boots

IN THE HIGHWAYS and byways of Scotland and Ireland you will meet up with many a strange and wonderful character, and with many a strange and wonderful tale. For those who love a story and keep the eye and heart of childhood that is sure, and doubly sure. Then you may well chance to meet with the folk beyond the invisible veil between our world and the otherworld, with elfin or fairy folk, or the nameless ones who trawl the dark.

It is how you welcome or treat these folk that they will visit you with dark mischief, or bright fortune, or mayhap, the treasure of a fine tale. These folk come in many guises as the ancient Celtic rune so wisely knows:

> Yestreen, a stranger was at my door.
> I put food in the eating place,
> drink in the drinking place,
> story music, and song in the listening place.
> And the stranger, he blessed myself, my house,
> my cattle and my dear ones.
> "For often, often, often," sings the lark in her song
> "goes the Lord in the stranger's guise."

And my friend, the traveller Duncan Williamson, a man of a thousand stories and songs, always said: 'A stranger is just a friend you have never met.'

It was from Duncan that I first heard the tale of the tramp, and yet in the strangest way did I not meet the same tale on my journey one happy year in the winding ways of green Ireland. It was Midsummer's Day, a sunny day, of a dusty afternoon, the sun hot, the day dry, I sat in a little leafy lane on a fallen log of wood. I was a little weary, having spent a day in the timeless land of tales that I was telling in a little village school to the bright eyes and eager ears of nine-year-olds.

As there I sat I saw coming my way an old man; tired he looked, and as he came closer I saw he was in rags, was weary by the step of him, and as he came closer still I saw there were tears, damp tears, upon his cheek. He seemed to be a tramp, a beggar-man, an old beggar-man.

I made to dip into my sporran, for I always wear the kilt, and said, 'Old man, can I give you something to buy yourself a bite to eat?'

'No thank you, sir,' said he.

'To get yourself something then to drink?'

'No, thank you, sir,' said he.

'You do not seem happy,' said I.

'No,' said he, 'I am not happy. It is Midsummer's day.'

'The day is beautiful,' I said, 'why on such a day are you not happy?'

'What is your name?' he asked, almost fierce.

'David Campbell,' I replied.

'What are you doin' here? You're not an Irishman.'

'No,' said I, 'I'm telling stories here. I'm from Scotland.'

'A storyteller,' said he, and paused a long time. 'Are you wantin' to know the story why I am not happy today?'

'I would,' said I.

'Do you mind if I sit there beside you on that log?'

'Please do,' I gestured, and he settled beside me and told me the tale.

On such a day as this he was walking the hard road; dusty it was and he dry and hungry and tired. That very day his way had taken him to a great mansion house standing apart from the road. 'Folk with plenty!' he thought and knocked on the big front door. To the door came a beautiful woman, dressed in a fine silk gown.

'Could you spare a little water, or a cup of tea, to a weary travelling man?' he asked.

'Get out before I set the dogs on you!' she snarled and slammed the door hard in his face.

And but the day before he came upon another stately house of fine stone with an avenue of trees. He came to the door, rang the bell, and heard it echo within the spacious hall. At length a portly man, big bellied, came. 'Ah,' thought the beggar-man, 'no shortage here of food for sure.'

'Could you spare a crust of bread,' said he, 'for a hungry traveller man?'

'I'll give you two minutes to be down that drive before I blow a hole in your backside,' said he. 'Shift! Move! Go!' The beggar-man left fast, as his legs would go, and leapt in fright as the door banged behind him like a gunshot.

He slept in a ditch and woke to another hot and sunny day, Midsummer's Day. Weary, thirsty, hungry, he walked the dusty road until the sole fell off one of his old worn boots and as he hobbled on, each step was as if pins and needles stabbed his foot. 'I'll need to rest,' he thought. 'I'm hungry, thirsty, and now this foot is scratched and bleeding.'

At that moment he reached a soft and grassy knoll, and there lay down. It was like a royal bed, and there at ease he lay. A beautiful butterfly fluttered by and then a big bumble bee came buzz-buzz-buzzing by, making a snoozy droning in the softness of the air. The beggar-man closed his eyes and slept.

In that sleep he had a wonderful dream. He dreamed he sat at a table covered with a cloth of Irish linen, white and shining. On the table was a spread of food fit for Irish kings; as he sat surveying the dishes of mouth-watering delicacies a tall man dressed in a suit of bluest blue approached bearing a golden goblet. 'This drink is for you,' he announced.

The tramp was faint with thirst as the servant lifted the rim to his mouth. At that moment a sharp impatient voice spoke out, 'Get up, get out, go!'

And the beggar-man awoke, found himself on the grassy knoll puzzled by the dream and by the vividness of this voice. Where did the voice come from? He looked everywhere around, and could see no sign of any one. Just then came fluttering by the many coloured butterfly and his old friend the big bumble bee, buzz, buzz buzzing, and to that lulling sound once more he fell asleep. Once more he had the identical dream.

At the linen covered table he sat. The spread as sumptuous as before. Once more the tall and blue-clad servant man appeared, and once more proffered the brimming golden goblet to his lips, and at the very moment he would drink and slake his thirst came that insistent, sharp imperious voice, loud, clear, 'Get up, get out, go!'

At once wide awake, he looked in every direction, up and down, saw no one. Was it the landowner? Was he trespassing? Was it the police? Worse, was it a voice in his own head? Thirsty he was, hungry, his foot bleeding and now was he losing his wits? 'Sleep, I must sleep,' he thought and closed his eyes.

Not a blink were they closed when came that little voice again, sharper, more insistent, 'Get up, get out, go!'

He was wide awake. Someone was here. The voice belonged to someone, or he was losing his wits? Alarmed, he looked high and low and all around, and then the voice spoke, distinct and clear, 'I'm down here!'

He could not believe his eyes. There at his feet, stood a little man, no taller than a foot. Bright blue, sky blue eyes he had, wore a hat with a jaunty feather, a waistcoat of leather, a green leather. He looked for all the world like an elf. He looked resolutely, straight, and fearlessly, into the face of the tramp, 'Get up, get out and go!' he said plainly.

'You look,' said the tramp, 'like an elf. I didn't believe you people existed.'

'Never mind what you believe,' said the cocky little fellow. 'Leave, get up, get out, go!'

'But,' said the tramp, 'if you people exist . . . '

The little man frowned. 'I'm not interested in your ifs. I'm here and I am telling you to go. Now!'

'But,' said the beggar-man, 'I thought elf people were supposed to be kind. Look at me, I'm tired, I'm hungry, I'm thirsty, and my foot is bleeding!'

Suddenly the little fellow's face grew soft, his eyes gentle, 'Very well,' said he, 'what could I give you to have you leave? Now!'

The tramp thought. His throat was saying, 'A drink, something to drink.' His stomach, 'Some food, something to eat.' Then his eye fell upon the little elf's boots, they were beautiful leather boots, neat, shiny, and with all the appearance of comfort. 'If I had boots like them!' he said, 'I would go.'

'Promise,' said the wee fellow, 'promise!'

'Yes, promise!' said the tramp.

'Promise?' said the elf.

'Yes, yes, yes, promise,' said the tramp.

'You have said it,' said the elf. There was a little whoosh, a swirl like a breath of wind in the grass, and when the beggar man looked again he was gone. The little elf man was gone.

'Did this happen? Was he really here, an elf,' thought the tramp, 'or am I losing my mind? Are my wits gone?'

Just then came the little voice. 'Here you are!' The beggar man looked down and there was the little fellow swinging something very small to and fro like a pendulum.

'What is that?' said the beggar.

'Your boots, these are your boots!'

The tramp knew not to laugh or cry. 'Don't be silly, don't make a fool of an old tramp man. These would not fit my pinkie, my little finger.' For indeed they were boots, tiny, neat, wonderful, boots.

'These are your boots,' replied the elf.

'I wish you would stop saying that,' said the tramp. 'Never till the end of time would these boots fit me.'

'These are your boots!'

The tramp was getting angry. 'Stop that; making a fool of me you are!'

'Watch and see,' said the elf, and there came a tiny little sound like the squeak of a bat, and the little fellow placed the boots on the ground and began to move his forefinger along their length. As he did so they grew. He snapped his fingers, and lo and behold, they were a fine pair of boots. The little sound ceased. 'These are your boots,' said he.

'They look a little, still on the small side,' said the tramp not meaning to sound ungrateful.

The little fellow sighed an elf weary sigh and said, 'These are elf boots, bigger on the inside than they are on the outside.' The tramp's brow furrowed. 'You wouldn't understand elf mathematics,' said the little man. 'Ask no questions, try these on.'

The tramp shuffled off his old boots, so old and tattered that they almost fell off by themselves. He put his foot into a boot, 'Oh, oh,' so soft and comfortable it was and the other the same. 'I could walk the world in these,' he thought, 'could dance, almost, I could fly in these.' He stood up and began to diddle and do a little Irish dance, like a man in the days of his youth. 'Oho!'

'You like the boots?'

'I love the boots, best I ever had. Thank you, a thousand thank yous.'

Suddenly the little man looked grave. 'These boots are a present from the elf king on his birthday, Midsummer's Day. If ever you tell where you got these boots you will never wear them again. Never tell. Promise.' Once more, three times, the little man demanded the promise, and then once more, with a sound like the whisper of wind in the grass, he was gone.

The beggar man stood up, he looked round. Truly the little man was gone. Was it a dream? He looked down. Cast aside were his battered and tattered boots, on his feet the beautiful boots. He diddled a tune and danced his way down the road, forgetting thirst and hunger.

The first person he met looked at him said, 'You look very happy, beggar man, would you like a little cup of tea?'

'O,' said he, 'a cup of tea would be fine for me!'

The second person he met said, 'Hey, old man, you look very merry, would you like a little beer?'

'Thankee, thankee,' said he, 'I've not had a beer for a year!'

Then an old woman he met, 'You are happy,' said she, 'would you like a little bit of toast?'

'O,' said he, 'a bit of toast would be the most!'

Further on a man greeted him on his cheerful way and said, 'Would you like a bit of pie?'

'I could die for a pie!' said he. And round the countryside he was known as the happy tramp. For the first time in his life he grew a little belly.

He sat back on the log and was silent. I looked at him and there running down his cheeks were tears.

'I thought you were happy,' I said.

'It was the happiest year of my life,' he answered.

'What happened?' He told me the end of the story.

It was a year from the time of his meeting with the little man, a year from the time of his gift of boots from the elf king. Looking at the boots he saw they were as new, not a scratch upon them. Never had he tired feet, never a bruise, or blister, and in all that long year never once had he taken the boots from his feet, not night nor day.

'I'm not being fair to these boots,' he thought. 'They deserve clean feet. So down to the riverside he went, removed the boots and placed them carefully by his side.

The reek of his feet sent even the flies buzzing away. Cows in the nearby field moved as far as they could. He dipped his feet in the cool water and even the fishes swam away but soon the water lapped his feet cool, and fresh, and clean. He leaned against the bank and closed his eyes. Life was sweet!

Suddenly a voice, 'Whose boots are these?' It was a fisherman in a little boat on the river.

'My boots,' answered he. 'These are my boots!'

'These are never a beggar's boots! I think you stole these boots.'

'Call me beggar, tramp, or what you will, but a thief I am not, I never stole nothing in my life.'

'These are never a beggar's boots. These boots are fit for a king,' said the fisherman.

The beggar was angry, 'Of course, they are fit for a king: they was given to me by the elf king on his birthday!'

The fisherman laughed. 'Elf! Elf king! Who ever heard of an elf king!' And he rowed on down the river.

'Some people,' thought the tramp, 'will not believe the truth when they hear it,' and at that moment he heard a high-pitched little sound like the squeaking of bats, and looking down, there before his eyes the boots were shrinking, growing smaller and smaller, and he seemed to hear in the breeze a little voice, 'And if you ever tell any one where you got these boots, you will never wear them again. He heard a click, like little fingers clicking, and a sigh, or was it the wind? The boots were tiny, not large enough to fit his pinkie, his little finger. Tears sprang into his eyes.

I looked at my old friend the beggar man sitting on the log beside me, 'And so,' said I, 'what did you do?'

'What could I do? I walked to the nearest village. My feet were cut and bleeding.'

'But the boots, the elf's boots, what did you do with them?'

'I kept them,' said he, 'and that is why my eyes are wet today, Midsummer's Day. Every Midsummer's Day I take them out of my bag and look at them and the tears start.'

Then he looked at me. 'David Campbell,' he said, 'you say you are a storyteller.'

'Yes.'

'What's that thing?' said he pointing at my sporran.

'It's my sporran, a purse for the kilt.'

'What do you keep in it?'

'Oh,' said I, 'a little money, a hanky, stories.'

'If I was to give you these boots,' said he, 'would you tell people my story? It would make me feel better.'

'Yes, I would do that,' said I.

'Promise?'

'Promise!'

'Open up that thing.' I opened my sporran and maybe not as surprised as you would think, saw him take out a tiny boot and drop it into my sporran. 'Promise?'

'Promise!

He took out the other little boot and it too he dropped in, 'Promise?'

'Promise!'

'I'm for the road,' he said, and rose. 'Good-bye, David Campbell, tell my story.'

'Wait,' I said, 'wait a moment. Would it be all right if I showed people these boots?'

He seemed to be listening. 'If they seem to be the right people,' he said, 'show them, but never let any one touch them, or what would happen to them I do not know. Thank you, sir.' And I watched him whistle and diddle his way down the summer road.

True to my word I kept the boots. I had inside my sporran a little sporran made, to keep the boots safe. When it seems the right time, and the right people, I tell the tramp's story and show people the boots, if they will come out of the little sporran inside the sporran, for this is a tale within a tale; it came from somewhere to my friend Duncan, and it seems if you are the one, you too will meet a beggar-man with such a tale to tell, just as I did.

The Ring of Brodgar

A MYSTERY SURROUNDS the circle of stones that form the Ring of Brodgar. But as the great Orkney writer George Mackay Brown has said, 'Orcadians of three or four generations ago had no doubt as to how they came to be there.'

Long, long ago, before our times, before the Viking times, before the time of the people who lived amongst the stones, at a time when memory itself creeps into the mists, there lived in Orkney a race of giants, great big blundering, stupid, fighting creatures. They did their business and held their rituals by night, for they had heard that the touch of the sun was death to them. And so in the daytime, the hours of light, they hid themselves under the earth in the safe and secret dark. How exactly they vanished, no one knows for sure, but legend has it, and story tells, that wild was their last night in celebration.

From sunset on this night of nights, the night of the midwinter solstice, their ritual dance was to last till just before the break of day, before the first low gleam of the sun glanced over the rim of the sea. Great was the drinking on this longest night. The giantess who brewed the heather ale, and the heady mead, was the daughter of the legendary giant, Cubbie Roo, of the Island of Wyre. Never was her ale stronger, never her dark mead sweeter to the tongue. All the giants in Orkney were gathered there that night and they gulped down boar's head after boar's head of that heather ale and that dark mead. Their roars of glee were like thunderous rollings on the sea. The thumping of their feet sent tremors over the earth, tidal waves over the ocean.

Dance followed dance through the dark hours of the night, ever faster, ever more furious, the music from their pipes like a howling tempest. Round and round the great circle whirled, wilder and wilder the heedless dancers flew, until the soberest of the blundering giants sensed the first greyness creeping into the dark, the first gleam on the rim of the western sea and lurched homewards.

'Time to be gone,' he roared and a few groggy companions followed him, stumbling towards Maeshowe and the Loch of Stenness, and across the island towards their homes. But the frenzy of the drink and the dance was on them.

'Not even the sun will stop our dance,' roared out Brodgar, the leader and the strongest of the giants, he alone, whose name comes down to us, as he swept the remaining dancers, round and round in a frenzy of madness . . .

The sun rose and turned every giant in Orkney to stone. There they stand still, caught by the rays of the morning sun, petrified for all time. Brodgar and his circle of dancers, caught and held as they were on their last living night on earth.

One, the tallest of them, was standing by the Loch of Stenness in the half light thinking how delicious would be a drink of the cold loch water after all the heavy dark mead, when a sunbeam turned him to stone. The gods are merciful in the case of that giant. Each New Year's morning he is allowed to stoop and take a sip of the cool waters of Loch Stenness. Others of these long gone giants you can see straggled across the island, lonely figures frozen to stone where they were sun struck to silence on their last journey home.

Betty Corrigall

'NO,' SAID BETTY CORRIGALL, 'I won't go for a walk with you. Never.'

But at the week's end she walked with the sailor called Willie as far as the shore of Moness in North Hoy. 'Kiss you!' said Betty Corrigall. 'What way would I kiss you, when I don't like you all that very much?'

And they walked one evening as far as the sea valley of Rackwick. A slip of moon rose over the hill, a silver shaving. All the Rackwick crofters and fishermen and their folk were inside. There were sixteen lighted windows and one dark window, where an old man had died the month before. At the edge of an oatfield the sailor kissed Betty Corrigall.

'I'll marry you,' said the sailor. 'I'll give up whaling, I'll build a house for both of us. I've enough money to rent a field at Crockness. There will be two cows, twenty sheep and a hundred hens. I'm good with saw and hammer and nails. There'll be a bed and a table, three chairs and a deep cupboard. I'll make a cradle that rocks. A star will shine on the doorstep.'

Betty said, 'I'd like that.'

And he put a storm of kissings and caressings about her face, and neck, and golden hair. And Betty Corrigall, she put a dewfall of kisses on his cheek, and mouth.

Then, about the middle of summer, it happened one morning that Betty Corrigall was sick. 'I think the milk last night was sour,' said her mother.

But in the week that followed, the milk on their porridge at supper-time was sweet and warm and good from Katie the cow; and every morning Betty was sick. Her mother put a bitter look on her. Her father said nothing. He went out and looked at the tall green oats growing beside the house.

'Willie Sinclair, he's wanting to marry me,' said Betty Corrigall. 'He's going to rent a field at Crockness. He'll build a house and make the furniture with his own hands. He's been to the factor to get permission, and to settle about the rent.'

'It's not before time,' said Betty Corrigall's mother. 'He should have made a start months ago. He should be carting the stones now.'

Betty Corrigall's father said it wasn't often a sailor made a good crofter. 'But still,' he had to admit, 'Willie Sinclair's father had been a hard-working man. You could do worse. I suppose,' said her father.

'They've made a bad beginning,' cried Betty Corrigall's mother. 'Let them make sure it doesn't come to a worse end! The way things are, this house is disgraced already. Never till this day did I know my daughter was a slut. The sooner you're out of this house and under that sailor's roof the better it'll be for everybody.'

The father said that if there was no heavy rain, or a gale between now and August, it would turn out to be a good enough harvest in his opinion. Betty Corrigall said that she and Willie Sinclair would have a good life together. She said, so low that her parents could hardly hear her, that she loved him with all her heart.

'The first wooden thing that man had better make,' said Betty's mother, 'is the cradle.'

After the corn began to hang heavy golden heads Betty did not put her face out-of-doors, both because she did not want her ripeness to be seen by the Hoy folk, and also because her mother blackly forbade her – not even to go to the well for water, nor even to drive Katie the cow from the unsickled oats. But her father secretly left the door unbarred at night, a thing he had never done before.

Night after night Betty Corrigall and her lover mingled dark whispers, moon-touched whispers, wondering silences. 'Yes,' Willie the sailor assured her, the factor had agreed to lease him the ten acres for a fair rent. 'Yes, yes,' he had already taken three cart-loads of stone from the quarry to the site of the croft. With great labour, for the place was stony, he had laid a foundation. He had bought enough planks and spars to make the door, window-frames, table, cupboard, bed.

'Make the cradle first,' said Betty. 'Make the crib quickly' . . .

The blacksmith had agreed to make him a plough. He was

negotiating with the farmer at Bu farm about the purchase of a young ox. And he kissed Betty Corrigall on her cold mouth. And the darkness took him; and Betty crept inside and barred the door and went into her little lamp-splashed room, until she lost herself soon in the sweet darkness of sleep.

Betty's mother waited until her husband went out to the barn. Then she said, 'It will have to be done quietly. I have spoken to the minister. There will be two witnesses, nobody else. I've made a wide gray coat for you to wear. The marriage is to be in the Manse. I suppose that man's mother – the slut that she is – will have to be there. And there's to be no drinking or dancing of fiddle-music afterwards.'

Betty Corrigall thanked her mother for having made the arrangements. She herself wanted no more. And that night Betty Corrigall waited at the gable-end of the croft. The moon was on the wane. Willie Sinclair did not come that night. Betty had wanted very much to unfold the marriage arrangements, also to know what progress was being made with the new croft. Nor did he come the next night, under the cold ember of the moon.

Betty Corrigall stood there three more nights, the last one an utter blackness without a star. The sailor had not come.

'Field? A field at Crockness?' said the factor to Tom Corrigall, Betty's father. 'I know nothing about a ten-acre field at Crockness. There's no land at Crockness available. What did you say the young man's name was? William Sinclair. A sailor. I don't know the man. There's a whaling man who's drunk every other night in this ale-house and that. That must be the man. A great teller of tall stories. A great womanizer, so I'm told. Yes, Sinclair's the name – now I remember. Arabella, poor woman, is his mother. I assure you, Tom, even if there was land available, I wouldn't rent a single yard to a fellow like that. No, he hasn't carted a single stone from the quarry – never asked – wouldn't get permission if he did.'

Betty Corrigall's father, after leaving the factor's office, stood in need of a drink. He dropped in at the ale-house at North Ness. Casually, over drams, he mentioned the name of Willie Sinclair the sailor to Mark the ale-house keeper.

'Ah, gone,' said Mark, 'cleared out, four days ago. The Yankee ship at Longhope, they signed him on. Bound for Russia, a cargo of grain and clocks. I'm not sorry to see the back of him. He owes me for two bottles of malt – I'll never see that money. I don't grudge it, so long as he doesn't come back here in a hurry. A liar, Tom, a fighter, a trouble-maker, couldn't hold his drink. I hope the bosun of that Yankee ship is a hard man.'

Tom Corrigall drank too many drams of malt that afternoon. Then he went home and struck his daughter hard across the face. A few words blazed like stars in his mouth; sufficient of them to indicate to the appalled woman and the quiet girl how matters stood with regard to Willie Sinclair the sailor, and Betty, and the unborn child, and the house that would be built of wind and sun and rain.

'The door's open,' he shouted to Betty Corrigall at last. 'Go!' and Betty Corrigall went out into the first silver flakes of winter.

Of course the crofter, once he had a good supper of boiled mutton and mashed tatties and neeps in him, was sorry for the things he had done and said, partly out of shock, partly from the fires of whisky he had kindled inside himself; black flames. He put on his coat, for it was a cold night in early winter, and a few snowflakes drifted like darkling moths athwart the window. Surely the girl would be at the end of the house, crying perhaps – but quietly, for Betty had never since childhood made wild demonstrations of either grief or joy.

She was not at the gable-end, shawled against the thickening snowflake-swarm. She was not in barn, or stable, or byre, nor over by the well where she loved to linger, listening to the songs of the sweet water deep down, bending to the fugitive gleams and glooms. Betty Corrigall was at no croft or farm or cottage in the district. No one had seen her. The father spent a whole night knocking on angry, or blank, or anxious doors. He even went to the sailor's mother's house, just at jet-and-russet dawn.

'Here?' said Arabella Sinclair in the cold door. 'No, Betty's not here. I wish she was here. I would have a good daughter at my fire and board. But no, I'm sorry. I haven't seen her for months. Oh yes, that's true enough, he left three or four days ago. It's been a quiet house since. I hope you have good word of Betty, and that soon. I love that girl better than the son I bore, and that's the truth.'

Nor was she at the Manse or the factor's or the schoolhouse; places where wisdom might have mended the troubles of a breached household. The man turned for home after the last door was closed against him.

As his feet slurred through the melting snow, going on the road that skirts the bay at Lyrawa, he saw two fishermen standing at the shore. He knew them; he waved a tired greeting in their direction. The elder fisherman held up his hand in such a way that it seemed to be a gesture of beseechment and of denial: 'Keep away!' The younger fisherman half-turned and then looked down again at a shape in the ebb. His spread hand hung white as a star above it. The body lay face down in a sea-brimmed cleft. But there was no mistaking the spread of golden hair.

Oh, it was unthinkable! – a suicide, and a child-burdened suicide at that, to lie amongst decent men, and women, and children, in the kirkyard – in God's acre. Neither the kirk session of Voes parish nor the kirk session of Hoy parish would countenance such an intrusion.

A few folk thought it a pitiable business. The girl had gone out of her mind with grief – in such circumstances the word 'suicide' had little meaning. A few others said that, muffled in a snow cloud, she had lost her way and gone over the shallow cliff. And others said she must have gone down to the shore, to see if she could see the American ship dipping between the islands at dawn; and the cold had seized her heart, she was bound to be delicate in her condition; and she had fallen into a rock pool, and was probably dead before the water closed over her . . .

It availed nothing, such talk. A hole was dug for Betty Corrigall in the moor, exactly on the border of the two parishes. The gravedigger consulted a map of Hoy with a thin line going across it, then sank in his spade again. And there the gravedigger and the father let down the sodden body of Betty Corrigall, with her head in Voes parish and her feet in Hoy parish. Then the gravedigger lit his pipe on the windy moor, and the father opened a whisky flask and passed it to him.

And while that generation of islanders withered slowly into death, one after the other, and after death rotted more urgently until they achieved the cleanness of skeletons, the deep peat moss kept the body of Betty Corrigall as pure and pristine as it had been in her youth.

Soldiers in the Second World War, digging drains in the moor, came on the body of Betty Corrigall as it lay crosswise with the line of the two parishes. The young men looked with wonderment into a face that had lingered sweet and beautiful from, it seemed, the first springs of time.

The Secret of Heather Ale

NOT A PEOPLE OF great height but doughty, and sturdy, and tough, and courageous, were the Pictish folk of the southwest corner of Alba: small and dark and strong. Long they could feast after hunt or victory in battle and great the drinking of their heather ale, a brew potent to put fleetness in the dance, music in the song, courage in the heart, and golden speech upon the tongue. Jealously was the secret recipe of that heather ale guarded, passed by word of mouth from father to son, and father to son down countless generations. Carefully guarded the secret of its making, for did not the quaffing of their heady ale open the pathway to a lover's heart, the doorways to other worlds, and to that place where the passing of many days was as the hearing of a little song. No one knew from whence it came, but it was believed to be a gift from the very goddess Danu at the time her own people held sway and power in Erin of ancient times. For certain it put a trance of seeing upon a man, remembrance of things past, making things present dew-drop clear and showing glimpses, like bright shadows, of things yet to be.

On a night when the first pangs of winter clawed the air was a mighty feast. In the daylong hunt a wild boar was taken, rites of celebration made, and now fire-roasted, it gave meat and magic power to all that little clan of Pictish folk. To join him at the fireside the old chief summoned his son who stood yet at the doorway of man-hood, not yet tested in the spear thrust of battle. In his strong hands the old man held the boarshead quaich abrim with heather ale. This he passed round, first to the hunter warriors, the women, the children, his son, and last himself. The old man's eyes were mist. He looked upon his son and yet before and beyond him too.

'I see a great battle is before us,' he said. 'The Scotti gather forces. We are few, they many. Our people will not outlive that day.' He, last to drink, quaffed down the ale and laughing loud into the night, his face a firelit glow, shouted into the wind, 'The secret of this ale their chief has coveted, they will not have. With us that sacred secret dies.'

As the old chief had seen in the flames of the feast fire by the working of the heather ale, so it was. At the day's end of the terrible battle with the host of the Scotti, no Pictish man stood but himself and his young son. The two stood surrounded on a clifftop high above a tumbling sea. Exhausted and encircled by the victorious warriors of the Scotti, they had fought until they could fight no more. The lofty leader of the Scotti tribe approached.

'One thing buys your lives,' said he. 'That thing you know for it is famed in all the land. I would know the secret of the heather ale. Freely spoken or by force I will have it. Choose!'

At that the old Pict spoke. 'Give me your ear alone,' said he.

'Bring him forward,' said the Scotti chief and into his ear the old one softly spoke: 'Great shame is on me if before my son I tell the making of this ale, for from the very goddess of our people has it come. And so I ask that you bind with thongs the boy and throw him from the cliff into the sea! I will not lose my honour in his eyes.'

The Scotti chief was much surprised but it was done, the young lad bound and from the clifftop thrown into the turmoil of the sea that crashed into the rock face far below.

'Do with me what you will,' said the old Pictish chief. 'From my untried son your force or guile might have torn our people's secret of the ale, but from me you never shall.'

At this the Scotti chieftain laughed. He laughed out loud and long, long and loud, he laughed while all stood silent by. Out of that shimmering stillness at last he spoke.

'Old man, your battle mettle in the spear rush I have admired. Yet it was little to this arrow you put to your own heart. See the well of tears that wets my eyes. They buy your life but, old fox, I cannot let you free to range and harry again my people.'

So it was that the last of the Pictish folk of the southwestern knuckle end of Alba was kept prisoner. A tale of his last days as captive still is told.

When he was old, blind, and not far from death some young

and boastful rebel warriors of the Scotti were thrown in to the prison where he lay. They were bragging of their feats of strength, their deeds in hunt and battle and seeing the old Pict lying on his bed of rushes began to taunt him, saying how puny were his people and their deeds beside those of the mighty Scotti.

Into the gloom the old man spoke. 'Let me feel the strength in your wrists,' said he. The strongest and the vainest into the old man's groping hand thrust the calf of his leg. 'That is but gristle,' said he, 'the Pictish folk are made of tougher stuff.'

The old man's hand, bony and lean, tightened and gripped, gave one sharp twisting wrench and snapped the bone as if it were a dried out twig. Was it the heather ale, gift to her people of the great goddess Danu that yet gave power to the old man's hand? Soon afterwards he died and with him forever the sacred secret of his people.

Blessing of the White Heather

IT WAS A DAY of bright Lughnasa, long and long ago. The people of the little highland village were early astir. A sweet sharp breeze blew from the sea. It was the day of the great boar hunt, a day that would, if fortune favoured, bring food to their bellies and a ceilidh fire of celebration with music, song and dance to the night. The clan chief was proud and mettlesome, the ferocity of his spirit matching that of his quarry, the great boar of Celyddon. Tall he sat upon his cross-bred steed, clansmen hunters around him, the women and children gathered to put propitious hunting on their day.

One old woman, a face like autumn oak leaves, brown and lined, came forward, a crow's croak in her throat, 'I bring a token, a handsel to bring good luck on your hunt.'

'Take yourself off,' laughed the proud chief, 'my fortune is here in this spear blade. Keep your tokens for your cailleach's tales.' And down the glen he rode, his hunter warriors at heel.

Not long it was when before them rose a great black boar, and in full cry, the hunger of the hunt upon them, they followed. Soon all fell behind but the chief, in feverous chase. Along the sea-cliff's margins above the swirling sea, thundered the mighty beast, then at the edge turned and charged the hunter's horse, which reared and threw the rider who tumbled rolling over the face of that high cliff's edge.

In the glen, and in her little black house, the cailleach gripped fast the token in her hand as if her hand were a wolf's teeth fastened on its prey.

A ledge broke the hunter's fall and there he clasped a large bush, holding fast to a tangled sod of heather, in hope that it would keep him from that fall into the foaming sea. Hearing the whinny of the horse his clansmen gathered at the cliff top, heard the cries of their chief and peering over the sheer precipice saw him clinging desperately to that heather clump. They lowered down ropes of carlin heather and drew their chief to safety. In his hand he held it, as if

164

it were his grasp on life, the flower, white flowers of heather. And it is told that on the homeward way they made a mighty hunt and took the wild boar.

Around the fire was feasting of boar meat, heather ale, dance and song. As he sat contented in the fire flame glow the old cailleach came to him. She bore a sprig of white heather in her hand and whispered in his ear, 'This is the charm that kept you from the sea.'

The story of this boar hunt moved through the glens of Scotland, and today a sprig of white heather is everywhere an emblem of good luck. Why the white heather is lucky is a very old legend I heard from the great traveller storyteller, Duncan Williamson.

Notes and Resonances

1 Lore of the Fianna

In the proud and far back days of Britain and Ireland a legendary brotherhood named 'the Fianna' kept the shores of these islands free of the foot of any invader, defending the people while not ruling them. Bands of warrior-hunters under one leader were a social reality in the tribal kingdoms of Erin and Alba. And in the passing of a thousand years, one warrior king became the central hero of a large corpus of tales, the Fenian Cycle: Finn mac Cumhaill was Find, the poet-warrior-seer whose wisdom and foreknowledge was externalized by his chewing tooth with thumb. He led seven battalions, known as the Fianna Éireann. With a striking power of compression and clarity, the heart of Finn is enshrined in the epigram on generosity at the start of the greatest prose narrative in the cycle, *Tóraigheact Dhiarmada agus Ghráinne* 'The Pursuit of Diarmait and Gráinne'. How the newly wedded wife of Finn elopes with his best man Diarmad Ó Duibhne has been narrated in Old Irish tradition since the ninth century. *Beinn Ghulbain*, a peak in Co. Sligo is most often the locale of the wild boar hunt which killed Diarmad. But in our Scottish story the scene is Glenelg; *Gleann Eilge* in Old Gaelic, a district in the west of Inverness-shire named for Ireland. Here a tribe of Celtic Britons inhabited the rugged hill country: the Caledones were fearless hunters, extremely swift of foot, enduring hunger, and thirst, and every kind of hardship. Their famous quarry was the great black boar.

For the early Celts hunting the boar constitutes the most fundamental cult legend, the flesh of the pig prized above all other. At any feast the boar's thigh is the champion's portion. At the holy settlement of La Tène joints of pork accompany the burial of Celtic heroes. All the passions of hunting, feasting, fighting, and procreation for Celtic peoples are contained in the boar cult. Significant is the curse of Diarmad's life by a half brother in the form of a wild boar that will destroy him in the glen of the hunting. For although the leading member of Finn mac Cumhaill's Fianna was fostered in the holy tribe of the Tuatha Dé Danann by Angus Óg, the patronage of love and beauty cannot dispel the raven's shadow. One of the greatest lovers of early Irish literature, Diarmad Ó Duibhne, shows the extraordinary length a Fenian will go to prove true in 'Daughter of the King Under Wave'. In the well-known story of Celtic magic, 'The Love-Spot', supernatural events occur totally naturally. Descendants of Diarmad, the clan Campbell, can track the legendary origin of their name – *cam* 'a female blind of an eye' refers to the power of the love-spot to ill-direct women. *Cam-bheul* 'distorted mouth' in Scottish Gaelic may owe its seed to the 'savage, crooked snout' of the pagan Irish boar that killed Diarmad at the base of Beinn Ghulbain; comparable to the boar with the same feature that killed Adonis in Greek mythology. The motif arises again with Osiris, killed by fighting a wild-boar, or a fierce rival king in disguise; and, according to Robert Graves, the crescent shaped tusks make the boar sacred to the Moon.

Throughout the Celtic world Cernunnos was the horned god and lord of nature, crowned with antlers of the stag. When the deer appears in stories there is commonly an engagement with the otherworld, realms of the Celtic imagination. Hunting the milk-white hind the hounds of Finn are charmed by the deer-mother Saba, who mates with Finn mac Cumhaill to produce his descendants Oisín and Oscar. The poetry of Oisín was so well loved and remembered that his songs have been recited as hymns by Gaelic singers to this day. The story of 'Oisín and Niam' dates back to Irish scripts from the eighth century where the power of the Celtic mind finds the realm of the heart beyond sorrow, old age and death in a language of pure spirit. The poet's inspiration is a goddess bestowing material and mental well-being.

Foundations were laid for the oldest written vernacular in Europe in Ireland with the arrival of the missionaries in the fifth century. Christian scribes wrote texts with a host of pagan elements sublimated under the cloak of the Living Christ. Legends of Saint Patrick, who wrote in Latin, show him abolishing paganism and the Celtic love of druidry. A marked feature of early religious narrative is affection for wild-life and wild nature, given full rein in 'Patrick of the Bells'. Part of the Fenian Cycle composed *c.*1200 is *Acallam na Senórach* 'the Colloquy of the Elders', a very famous argument waged by Oisín and St Patrick over the relative values of Christianity to the hunting culture. It is retold by David Campbell as 'Flyting'.

II Legends of the Saints

Missionary work during the second half of the sixth century by holy men and women in Celtic Scotland is recorded in stories that feature a very personal relationship felt with God. To mother a Christ-child was not a passion exclusive to Thenaw, in the story of Kentigern's birth; St Íde had a wish to nurse the infant Jesus in the form of a baby in her cell. No fewer than twenty five holy men in Scotland, all contemporaries of Colum Cille, became martyrs of Christianity; why the fervent religious activity? Christian leaders were themselves men of high birth, like the Celtic aristocracy. Their monastic sites were not chosen at random but were often in the vicinity of the local prince or king, who would give consent and lend protection. The genealogies of the saints came to be known and preserved because they belonged to ruling families. St Fillan, the first to bring Celtic Christianity to the heart of Caledonia was an Irish prince. Kentigern is the grandson of King Urien, a member of the great ruling family Coel Hen of Ayrshire and Galloway, Dumfriesshire and Carlisle; their descendants the princes of Lothian. In the story of 'The Ring' Kentigern saves the queen of Strathclyde; representing the second great branch of ruling Britons, Riderch Hael, during the fifth and sixth centuries from the Forth and Clyde isthmus to the Tyne. Known as *Gwyr y Gogledd* 'the Men of the North', these families were praised in Old Welsh poetry –

the fury of Urien like the tidal current of the Solway – noted for its violence. Sweet by terrible contrast is 'The Robin'. *The Life of St Kentigern* by Jocelinus, recorded the original form of Glasgow, *clas-gu* 'cloister dear' from the Welsh. Pagan, Celt, and Christian, saints are united in the forest of Goddeu, the final retreat for both Kentigern and Merlin. Now Lanarkshire, the district was once wholly covered with woods, apart from the heath on the mountain tops. At the foot of a thorn tree below the churchyard of Drumelzier Merlin is buried.

Invoked for the fragility of new life, Brìde of the Western Isles has many charms and incantations to her healing powers published in Carmichael's *Carmina Gadelica*. Her feast day is the first day of spring in the Celtic calendar, 1 February. In David Campbell's story of her arrival on Iona, the druid who received Dugall Donn and his young daughter was Fer hÍ mac Eogabail 'Son of Yew', his father Eo-gabal 'Yew-fork'. Formed through the magic of Fer hÍ, the yew-tree was a cult or divinity of the island Celts, not unattractive to a certain young Dove of the Church. As the third most celebrated saint in Ireland, after St Patrick and St Brigid, Columba shares a romantic, folkloric, past as the great-grandson of Conall Gulban, founder of the kingdom Tir Chonaill (Donegal). Historical realities of the saint's Christian mission are well chronicled; Columba established thirty eight monasteries in Ireland and another eight in Scotland, six in Dál Riada. The monastery founded in 563, Í-Choluim Chille on the island of Iona, is today a world centre for Christianity. The life of Colum Cille by David Campbell is told in nine stories based on oral versions and several published sources, prinicipally *Adomnán of Iona: Life of St Columba*. The Derry cry of lamentation in 'The Dream' is from Mannu O'Donnell's *The Life of Colum Cille*. The story of Moluag and Columba in verbal combat for the isle of Lismore was a legend told by Rev. D. Carmichael in *They built on Rock: Stories of the Celtic Saints*. Rosemary Thompson drawing on the second book of Adamnan, translated by Wentworth Huyshe, wrote earlier versions of 'Dair and Lugne' and the slave girl freed in 'Black Boar of Celyddon'. The confrontation of saint and wild boar on the isle of Skye symbolizes the religious conflict of Christian and Pict. Overcome in its tracks by non-violence the druid Broichan of the last Pictish King Brude must die. Current in South Skye oral tradition, along with 'Little Red Squirrel' and 'The Devil in Skye' is the legend of Chief McFhionghuin (Mackinnon) 'the tribe of Finn', who killed a boar by thrusting a bone though its snout.

III Celtic Folk and Fairy Tales

'A Door in the Wind' opens the third set of Celtic stories by David Campbell, who pays homage to the Gaelic history of the MacLeods of Morvern. As the grandson of The Very Reverend Norman MacLeod (1812–1872), a man who spent his life serving the cause of the Highland Gael, Lord George MacLeod is revered as the successor to Columba. His life story, told here by David Campbell, is based on the excellent biography of the Scottish peer by Ron Ferguson, together with diverse reflections on his father from Sir Maxwell MacLeod. Christianity is the foundation of Scotland, its history bound with the Church. Kenneth MacAlpin formed Alba, the new kingdom of Scotland in 844 by uniting Scotti and Pict. For three hundred years, since the time of Columba, the two groups of peoples had been racially distinct; their cultures, and religions, captured imaginatively by Robert Louis Stevenson in 'The Secret of Heather Ale'. His narrative poem has been returned to source as a Galloway legend in the story by David Campbell.

To evangelize the tribes of Alba was the aim of Christian holy men, but the Picts of Orkney and the Northern Isles remained pagan for many centuries after mainland conversions. Originally known as the Isles of Boars, Orkney was the home of George Mackay Brown, a writer of great natural strength. Bearing only the name of a girl, a gravestone on the boundary between Birsay and Harray spoke from the 'otherworld' to the Orcadian writer, to inspire his story of a pregnant girl's suicide. 'Betty Corrigall', taken from

Northern Lights: A Poet's Sources 1987, and can be heard read aloud by David Campbell on the CD *Orkney after Sunset: Tales and Tunes.*

The Celtic 'otherworld' is a realm beyond the senses, a world peopled by fairies who can be known through storytelling. In four stories David Campbell traces the origin of the fairy world, from Lady Gregory's testament, to the invasion of Ireland by Milesian Gaels (*c.*300 BC), to midsummer visions of the Fairy King and the Scottish travellers' belief today. 'Fairy Wind' was told by Michael Ross from Dublin who had it from a manuscript with these words: Eamonn a Búrc, Aill na Brón, Cill Chiaráin, Cáma, Conamara; and *he* heard it from his father fifty years ago.' The tale from Connemara, of West Co. Galway ended with the run, 'That's my story. If there's a lie it wasn't me that made it up. If there is a sin in it, let God sort it out.' Stories of the leannán sídhe, the 'fairy lover', are among the most dramatic and poetic of the lore from the Celtic otherworld. Sheila Quigley told David Campbell the version above. In 'Hunter of the Yellow Grouse', passed down to the author from Paraig MacNeil of Dunblane, the hill lover loses his soul, in attachment bringing home the truth of the Scottish Gaelic proverb, *Is e innleachd seilge a sìor leanmhuinn* 'the art of hunting is ever pursuing it'.

The collection of David Campbell's Celtic tales ends with 'Blessing of the White Heather' restoring the balance of man with nature. In the lore of poet and storyteller no other animal is more ferocious or heroic in defense than the boar. With its great sexual power the wild boar is not only a symbol of fertility, but also of the sacred ritual of hospitality. In Duncan Williamson's legend of the white heather, the great black boar brings a heathen chief to the edge of the world-non-world, where he is saved by the faith of the cailleach, the old woman of the woods. A sod of white heather growing on the cliff face of death is brought home and planted at the front of the boar lord's castle. Each year it spread and got bigger till the laird was able to give everyone a piece of it. Everyone who got a piece of that heather kept it, and then gave a piece to somebody else. The luck of the white heather spread far and wide, till today it's spread over three parts of the world. While the boar has been extinct for three hundred years in Britain, and worship of the three thousand-year-old boar god eradicated by the imposition of an absolute, supreme Trinity; the cult of the boar survives. Against all odds, nature prevails in the tales of the Celt.

Linda Williamson
Edinburgh 2009

Selected Bibliography

Adomnán of Iona: Life of St Columba (Penguin, 1995)

Black, R., ed. *The Gaelic Otherworld: John Gregorson Campbell's Superstitions of the Highlands & Islands of Scotland and Witchcraft & Second Sight in the Highlands & Islands* (Birlinn, 2005).

Brown, G.M. *Northern Lights: A Poet's Sources* (John Murray, 1999)

——. *An Orkney Tapestry*, 2nd ed. (Quartet Books, 1973)

——. *Portrait of Orkney*, 2nd ed. (London: John Murray, 1988)

——. *Winter Tales* (John Murray, 1995)

Bruford, A. and D.A. MacDonald. *Scottish Traditional Tales* (Edinburgh: Polygon, 1994)

Campbell, D., comp. *Tales to Tell* (Edinburgh: The Saint Andrew Press, 1986)

Carmichael, A. *Carmina Gadelica*, 6 vols (Edinburgh, 1900–71)

The Celts: Sacred Symbols (London: Thames and Hudson, 1995).

Dwelly, E., comp. *The Illustrated Gaelic-English Dictionary* (Glasgow: Gairm Publications, 1994)

Farmer, D., ed. *Oxford Dictionary of Saints,* 4th ed. (Oxford University Press, 1997)

Ferguson, R. *George Macleod: Founder of the Iona Community* (London: Collins, 1990)

Graves, R. *The Greek Myths* (London: The Folio Society, 1966)

Heaney, S. *Sweeney Astray* (London: Faber and Faber, 1983)

Jackson, K.H. *A Celtic Miscellany: Translations from the Celtic Literatures* (Penguin Books, 1971)

Lacey, B., ed. *The Life of Colum Cille* by Mannus O'Donnell (Dublin: Four Courts Press, 1998) the work *Betha Colaim Chille* composed in sixteenth century Irish Gaelic from folk traditions in Irish and foreign prose sources

Lady Gregory's Complete Irish Mythology (London: Octopus Publishing, 2004)

Lahr, J., ed. *Celtic Quest* (New York: Welcome, 1998)

Lamont, D.M. *Strath: In Isle of Skye* (Glasgow: Celtic Press, 1913) Skye Graphics 1984 reprint

MacCulloch, J.A. *Celtic Mythology* (New York: Dover, 2004 reprint of 1918)

MacKillop, J. *Dictionary of Celtic Mythology* (Oxford University Press, 1998)

MacLeod, G.F. *The Whole Earth Shall Cry Glory: Iona prayers by Rev. George F. MacLeod* (The Iona Community, 1985)

Mcneill, F. Marian. *An Iona Anthology* (Glasgow: The Iona Community, 1947)

Nicolson, A., ed. *A Collection of Gaelic Proverbs and Familiar Phrases,* 4th ed. (Edinburgh: Birlinn, 1996)

O'Flaherty, W.D. *Hindu Myths: A Sourcebook translated from the Sanskrit* (Penguin, 1975)

Ó hÓgáin, D. *Myth, Legend and Romance: An Encyclopaedia of the Irish Folk Tradition* (Prentice Hall Press, 1991).

Orkney After Sunset: Tales and Tunes CD by David Campbell and the Wriggley Sisters (Orkney Isles: Attic Records, 2001)

Rolleston, T.W. *Myths and Legends of the Celtic Race* (London: Constable, 1987 reprint of 1911)

Ross, A. *Pagan Celtic Britain: Studies in Iconography and Tradition* (London: Cardinal, 1974)

'A Selection of Scottish Lives of Saints' pamphlet reproduced by the School of Scottish Studies, University of Edinburgh, n.d.)

'St Columba' in *They Built on Rock: Stories of the Celtic Saints* (London: Hodder and Stoughton, 1948)

Thompson, R.C. *The Dove of the Church or Columcille* (Glasgow: Iona Community, 1980)

Watson, W.J. *The History of the Celtic Place-Names of Scotland* (Edinburgh: Birlinn, 2005 reprint of 1926)

Glossary

Words and names from Scots (Sc), Scottish Gaelic (ScG), Welsh (W), Irish (Ir), Old Irish (OIr), Gaulish (G) and Latin (L)

Alba Scotland (ScG); Britain in early Irish literature. Albion was the old name of Great Britain from albus 'white' (L), as in the Alps and 'White-land', given by the Celts of Gaul to the chalk cliffs of the south coast

Amergin warrior-poet who led Milesians, the invading Gaels of Mediterranean origin; father of lyrical poetry in Ireland

Angus Óg young Angus, son of youth (Ir), god of youth and beauty, poetry and music, among the Tuatha Dé Danann; child of the Dagda and Boyne River goddess; brings cows to Ireland from India with Manannán mac Lir; protector of several heroes including Diarmad of Fenian Cycle; important defence was cloak of invisibility

Arfderydd, Battle of 573/5 AD, when Gwenddolau, Welsh chieftain of the Old North (i.e. Scottish Lowlands) was slain, and victory taken by Rhydderch of Strathclyde. Site identified with Arthuret in Cumberlandshire on River Esk, north of Carlisle. In Welsh narratives this battle causes the madness of Merlin who, traumatized, flees to the forests of Caledonia, receives the gift of prophesy and lives in the trees with wild beasts for fifty years

ball seirce   love-spot, blemish (Ir) possessed by Diarmad Ó Duibhne which, when seen by a woman, would render her unable to love any other

borabu   horn of the Fianna, circled round like a seashell; its blast could summon warriors from all parts of Ireland at any time

bealach   mountain pass, glen (ScG)

Beinn Ghulbain   Ben Bulben, peak of razor shaped mountain in Co. Sligo rich in legendary and literary associations

Beltaine fires   bonfires on mountaintops to celebrate beginning of summer on Bealltuinn 'first day of May' (ScG)

Brehon   law specialist in early Ireland; Brehon Laws, textbooks of law records

Bride Bhìth   tranquil Brigid of the Isles (ScG); the very popular Irish St Brigid, abbess of Kildare, d. 525, venerated in Scotland, Wales, the Isle of Man and in England. In the Scottish Islands she is referred to as 'Mary of the Gael', the exemplar of virgins, midwife of the Virgin Mary; patron of poets and blacksmiths, carries on Celtic tradition of Brigit, the pre-Christian goddess of fire

Briton   Brython 'a Briton' (W), a Welshman. The two most important tribes of the Britons in the North are the Caledonians and the Maetae, who become divisions of the Picts by fourth century; Picts and Scots drove the Britons out up to River Tyne in the fifth century; at the beginning of the sixth they recovered

Caerlaverock	entrenched or stone-girt fort of Llywarch (W); erelc 'an ambush' (OIr)
cailleach	single woman, old woman, carline (ScG)
Campbell	cam-bheul: cam 'curved, deceitful, blind of an eye' and beul 'mouth; opening' (ScG)
carlin heather	sturdy, long-stemmed heather used to make ropes (Sc)
ceilidh	party, visit (ScG)
Celyddon	forest of the Celtic tribe Caledonii, who lived in the area from Loch Long to Beauly Firth, Caledonia, Scotland (W); primal forest of oak, hazel, ash, birch and pine where boar, elk and bear sustained the hunter-gatherers in the highlands of northern Britain. Base of name from kal 'cry' (W) and 'din, clamour' (Greek); like Calydon of Aetolia in Greece, the rocky hill country inhabited by tribe of Caledones was *called* 'hard' (W)
Celts	warrior tribes of Gaul who lived south and west of the Rhine, west of the Alps and north of the Pyrenees reaching greatest extent of influence in classical culture in the second and third centuries BC. The Celts of Gaul moved west and north into new territories, mingling with older populations; and in the first century Celtic tales were heard all over Britain, told by tribes of Britons, speaking a language like Gaulish and similar to Welsh. Of the thirty-five Celtic speaking tribes in Britain during the Roman occupation, eighteen were in Scotland. A ruling class, military aristocracy, among the native inhabitants of Britain and Ireland from

the third century BC, distinguished by their physique, tall, fair or ruddy-haired men, blue-eyed and large of limb; renowned by the Greeks as the barbarians of Europe, their Indo-European language, art, religious practices and vibrant literature came to be recorded in later centuries by Christian monks in Ireland, bearing a different branch of the Celtic language, and in more recent centuries by scholars of folklore from every nation

cenél   tribe, kindred (OIr)

clàrsach   Celtic harp (ScG)

Caílte   a nephew of Finn famed for athletic skills and fleetness of foot

Colum Cille   Columba 'dove' (L); cill 'church, cell' (Ir) patron saint of Scottish Gaelic Christianity, c.521–97. Born in Co. Donegal he claimed descent from Cathair Mór, king of Leinster. Baptized Crimthann but took the name Colum Cille through angelic intervention

Conn   Céthchathach 'of the hundred battles' (Ir) 177–212 AD, great conquering leader of intelligence; Irish province of Connacht named after him, Lords of the Isles, Clan Donald in Gaelic Scotland claim descent from him

Corrievreckan   Coire Bhreacáin 'whirlpool of the Breccán' (ScG) who was drowned with his company of fifty ships between Northern Ireland (the coast of Antrim) and Rathlin Island, now called Sloc na Mara

Cruachain	the great fortress of Connacht; also known as the cave of Crúachu and the ridge of the druids
Cúchulainn	greatest hero in early Irish literature, predominates in the Ulster Cycle (from seventh-century texts); characteristic quickness and small dark stature
curach	boat made of wicker and covered with skins or hides, coracle (ScG)
Dagda	good god (Ir) principal god of Old Irish tradition; skilled in many endeavours, a warrior, an artisan, a magician and an omniscient ruler; king of Tuatha Dé Danann who specializes in druidical magic
Dair	oak: Daron, goddess of the oak (Ir)
Dál Riada	Irish speaking kingdom of Scots in Argyll
Diarmait mac Cerbaill	high king of Ireland c.545–565, last pagan monarch
Diarmad Ó Duibhne	'the unenvious' (Ir) Irish Fenian hero of the Corcu Duibne sept of west Kerry; fostered in the holy tribe of the Tuatha Dé Danann by Angus Óg
Donn	dun brown; lord (Ir) name borne by kings, the ruler of the dead; an ancestor-deity. Donn Ó Duibhne is father of Fenian hero Diarmad whose vengeance causes son to be pursued by magical boar
Dord Fian	war chant or cry of the fianna of Finn mac Cumhaill; low on the musical scale, often delivered with a bass voice; dord (Ir) 'droning, intoning'

Druid	druwid 'wise man of the woods' (G); druí 'diviner'
Dubthach	name traditionally ascribed to Saint Brigid's father, identical with Dugall Donn, legendary father of St Brigid in Scottish Gaelic genealogies; dubh 'black, dark' (Ir)
dún/dùn	a fort, fortified place, royal residence (Ir/ScG); from dùnon (G), din (W)
Erin	variant of Ireland, twelfth-century use by King David of Scotland; Eire or Eriu 'Ireland' (ScG)
Fer Doirich	the dark druid who twice transformed Saba, mother of Oisín, into a fawn because she refused his love
fianna	bands of warrior-hunters living in the wilderness learning how to hunt and fight under one leader, the Fian-chief or king fian-warrior, possessor divination
Finn mac Cumhaill	'fair son of hazel' warrior king named for the hazelnuts of occult knowledge which he gleaned by tasting the salmon of wisdom that ate the nuts from the nine hazels growing over the Well of Sagais, common source of rivers Boyne and Shannon in Ireland
flyting	competition in verbal abuse (Sc), a contest of poets
geis	taboo or prohibition placed upon hero or prominent personage in Irish narratives, requiring positive demand or injunction, specifying forbidden or unlawful actions; guidhe 'request or prayer; curse' (ScG)

Gaidhealtachd	range of the Gaelic-speaking highlands (ScG)
Glenelg	glen of the pig (Old Gaelic)
Goll mac Morna	fiery foe of one eye, lost in battle leading killers of Finn's father
Gráinne	daughter of Irish king Cormac mac Airt who elopes with Diarmad Ó Duibhne while betrothed to Finn mac Cumhaill; grán 'grain; she who inspired terror' (Ir)
gulba	beak, sting (Ir); mouth (ScG)
Hill of Allen	home of Finn mac Cumhaill and the Fianna in Co. Kildare, today north-east of Kildare town
hirple	walk lamely, limp, move unevenly (Sc)
Í	island (OIr) Iona in early Celtic texts; Eu or Eo 'a yew-tree' (OIr)
Kepduf Hill	ceap dubh 'black block' (ScG) hill north-west of Dunpelder from where Kentigern's mother was thrown down; now called Kilduff
Kentigern	Cintu-pennos 'first head': cynben 'prince' (W); Lothian saint (d. 612), evangelist of Strathclyde and Cumbria
Languoreth	Queen of Rhydderch; langa 'lank female' (ScG); languoring wife
Lochlan	realm of dangerous invaders, often Norway
Lughnasa	third season of the Gaelic year beginning 1 August; harvest of first fruits
Lugne	lùgan 'a deformed, sorry looking fellow' (ScG); echoes Lug Lamfhota, old Irish sun god with wide hands and long arms

machair   extensive low-lying fertile plain; long sandy range fringing Atlantic side of the Outer Hebrides, closely covered with short green grass, thickly studded with herbs of fragrant odours and plants of lovely hues (ScG)

Merlin   sixth-century Arthurian magician and prophet, in Scottish Lowland tradition based on Lailoken, the hairy wild man of the woods

Moluag   saint of northern Ireland (c.530–92) founded the island monastery of Lismore

Munghu   Mungo 'dear, amiable' (W) Kentigern, patron saint of Glasgow

mùs e   that's too much (Ir)

Nesa   pre-Christian form of River Ness (ScG)

Niam   brightness, radiance (Ir) the lover of Oisín, leads to lengthy sojourn in the Land Of Youth

Oisín   'little deer' (Ir) prinicipal son of Finn mac Cumhaill, warrior and poet; father to Oscar

Oran   monk sacrificed on Columba's arrival in Iona

Orc   'young boar' (OIr) Sea of the Orcs was Pentland Firth in ninth century writings of Nennius; Inse Orc 'the Isles of Boars' used by Pytheas 300 BC ; Orcoi 'boars' tribal name of Picts inhabiting the thirty islands known as the Orcades, now Orkney

Oscar   deer-lover, os 'fawn' (Ir); bravest and most valourous of the Fianna, son of Oisín, grandson of Finn mac Cumhaill

Owain	son of King Urien and prince of Rheged, the province including Galloway, Dumfriesshire and Carlisle
Patrick	fifth-century bishop and apostle (d. 460), became Ireland's national saint
Picts	picti 'painted men' (L) earliest people in the British Isles to speak a Celtic language. Pretani 'figured folk' and Cruithni are P– and Q– Celtic words for the Picts, who tattooed as well as painted themselves and endowed Scotland with an artistic legacy of stylized carved memorial stones and crosses
quaich	bowl-shaped drinking cup (Sc)
quicken tree	rowan, favoured by druids, best protective agent
Rhydderch	Welsh king Riderch of Strathclyde (d. 570) much associated with stories of St Kentigern
sain	bless, heal (Sc)
Scotti	Celtic speaking invaders of Argyll from Ulster; Goidelic language of Scotti used by Celtic saints of Ireland to spread their teachings of Christ
seanachaidh	reciter of tales or stories; historian, genealogist (ScG)
sídh	fairy mound (OIr)
Thenaw	mother of St Kentigern, educated by St Monenna (d. 517)
thirled	bound by ties of affection (Sc)

Tir nan Òg   Land of Youth or the Ever-Young (ScG) most widely known of all the otherworldly lands from early Irish tradition, often perceived to be west of Ireland

Tuatha Dé   people, god-tribe, or nation of Ana (Ir), the

Danann   principal goddess of pre-Christian Ireland linked with Dana or Danu, mother goddess of the Danube Valley in Austria, home of the earliest Celtic tradition, the Halstatt culture of 1000 BC; 'land of Ana' the ninth-century name for Ireland

Some other books published by **LUATH** PRESS

Out of the Mists

John Barrington
ISBN 1 905222 33 5 PBK £8.99

In the earliest hours of the morning shepherds gather, waiting for the mists that conceal the hillsides to clear. To pass the time they tell tales of roaming giants, marauding monks and weird witches. Enter this world of magic and wonder in *Out of the Mists*, a delightful collection of stories which will captivate and entertain you while answering your questions about Scottish history and folklore.

Why did St Andrew become the patron saint of Scotland?

How can you protect yourself from faerie magic?

What happened to Scotland's last dragon?

John Barrington uses wit and his encyclopaedic knowledge of Scottish folklore to create a compelling collection of stories that will capture the imaginations of readers of all ages.

Luath Storyteller: Tales of Edinburgh Castle

Stuart McHardy
ISBN 1 905222 95 5 PBK £5.99

Who was the new-born baby found buried inside the castle walls?

Who sat down to the fateful Black Dinner?

Who was the last prisoner to be held in the dungeons of Edinburgh Castle, and what was his crime?

Towering above Edinburgh, on the core of an extinct volcano, sits a grand and forbidding fortress.

Edinburgh Castle is one of Scotland's most awe-inspiring and iconic landmarks. A site of human habitation since the Bronze Age, the ever-evolving structure has a rich and varied history and has been of crucial significance, militarily and strategically, for many hundreds of years.

Tales of Edinburgh Castle is a salute to the ancient tradition of storytelling and paints a vivid picture of the castle in bygone times, the rich and varied characters to whom it owes its notoriety, and its central role in Scotland's history and identity.

Luath Storyteller: Tales of the Picts

Stuart McHardy

ISBN 1 84282 097 4 PBK £5.99

For many centuries the people of Scotland have told stories of their ancestors, a mysterious tribe called the Picts. This ancient Celtic-speaking people, who fought off the might of the Roman Empire, are perhaps best known for their Symbol Stones – images carved into standing stones left scattered across Scotland, many of which have their own stories. Here for the first time these tales are gathered together with folk memories of bloody battles, chronicles of warriors and priestesses, saints and supernatural beings. From Shetland to the Border with England, these ancient memories of Scotland's original inhabitants have flourished since the nation's earliest days and now are told afresh, shedding new light on our ancient past.

Tales of the North Coast

Alan Temperley

ISBN 0 946487 18 9 PBK £8.99

Seals and shipwrecks, witches and fairies, curses and clearances, fact and fantasy – the authentic tales in this collection come straight from the heart of a small Highland community. *Tales of the North Coast* were collected in the early 1970s by Alan Temperley and young people at Farr Secondary School in Sutherland. All the stories were gathered from the area between the Kyle of Tongue and Strath Halladale, in scattered communities wonderfully rich in lore that had been passed on by word of mouth down the generations. The book also includes chilling eye-witness accounts of the notorious Strathnaver Clearances when tenants were given a few hours to pack up and get out of their homes, which were then burned to the ground.

Tall Tales from an Island [Mull]
Peter Macnab
ISBN 0 946487 07 3 PBK £8.99

Peter Macnab was reared on Mull, as was his father, and his grandfather before him. He heard many of these tales as a lad, and others he has listened to in later years.

There are humorous tales, grim tales, witty tales, tales of witchcraft, tales of love, tales of heroism, tales of treachery, historical tales and tales of yesteryear. There are unforgettable characters like Do'l Gorm, and philosophical roadman, and Calum nan Croig, the Gaelic storyteller whose highly developed art of convincing exaggeration mesmerised his listeners. There is a headless horseman, and a whole coven of witches. Heroes, fools, lairds, herdsmen, lovers and liars, dead men and live cats all have a place in this entrancing collection.

Some of these tales are discreetly transmitted in the... words of real or composite village personalities... others are from the Gaelic, most of them probably genuine, having lost nothing but gained a lot... during their passage down the generations from one oral raconteur to the next.

THE HERALD

The Supernatural Highlands
Francis Thompson
ISBN 0 946487 31 6 PBK £8.99

An authoritative exploration of the otherworld of the Highlander, happenings and beings hitherto thought to be outwith the ordinary forces of nature. A simple introduction to the way of life of rural Highland and Island communities, this new edition weaves a path through second sight, the evil eye, witchcraft, ghosts, fairies and other supernatural beings, offering new sightlines on areas of belief once dismissed as folklore and superstition.

Excellent guidebook to the Gaelic-speaking underworld.

THE HERALD

Details of these and other books published by Luath Press can be found at:
www.luath.co.uk

Luath Press Limited

committed to publishing well written books worth reading

LUATH PRESS takes its name from Robert Burns, whose little collie Luath (*Gael.*, swift or nimble) tripped up Jean Armour at a wedding and gave him the chance to speak to the woman who was to be his wife and the abiding love of his life. Burns called one of 'The Twa Dogs' Luath after Cuchullin's hunting dog in Ossian's *Fingal*. Luath Press was established in 1981 in the heart of Burns country, and is now based a few steps up the road from Burns' first lodgings on Edinburgh's Royal Mile.

Luath offers you distinctive writing with a hint of unexpected pleasures.

Most bookshops in the UK, the US, Canada, Australia, New Zealand and parts of Europe either carry our books in stock or can order them for you. To order direct from us, please send a £sterling cheque, postal order, international money order or your credit card details (number, address of cardholder and expiry date) to us at the address below. Please add post and packing as follows: UK – £1.00 per delivery address; overseas surface mail – £2.50 per delivery address; overseas airmail – £3.50 for the first book to each delivery address, plus £1.00 for each additional book by airmail to the same address. If your order is a gift, we will happily enclose your card or message at no extra charge.

Luath Press Limited
543/2 Castlehill
The Royal Mile
Edinburgh EH1 2ND
Scotland

Telephone: 0131 225 4326 (24 hours)
Fax: 0131 225 4324
email: sales@luath.co.uk
Website: www.luath.co.uk